Law and Rockets

An American Lawyer in Iraq

MICHAEL O'KANE

2016

ANDALUS PUBLISHING

Law and Rockets: An American Lawyer in Iraq
ISBN-13: 978-0-9910476-9-7
© 2016 Michael O'Kane

All rights reserved.
Printed in the United States of America. No part of this book may be used or reproduced in any manner without written permission except in the case of brief quotations embodied in critical articles and reviews. For information, address Andalus Publishing, 1507 7th Street Suite 392, Santa Monica, CA 90401 or admin@andaluspublishing.com.

Credits: Map of Security Incidents 2003-2009, *The Journal of ERW and Mine Action*, Issue 15.3 (Fall, 2011), ISSN: 2154-1485, used with permission. Photographs of Sabre Compound and Ops Center, © Brad Thompson, used with permission. Green Zone map provided by the U.S. Department of Defense. Other photographs © Michael O'Kane.

Library of Congress Publisher's Cataloging-in-Publication Data

Names: O'Kane, Michael, 1955-
Title: Law and rockets : an American lawyer in Iraq / Michael O'Kane.
Description: Santa Monica, CA : Andalus Publishing, [2016]
Identifiers: ISBN: 978-0-9910476-9-7
Subjects: LCSH: Lawyers, Foreign–Iraq–Baghdad–2003- –Biography. | Law firms–Iraq–Baghdad–2003- –History. | Practice of law–Iraq–Baghdad–2003- | Law–Iraq–History–2003- | Iraq–Politics and government–2003- | Iraq War, 2003-2011–Personal narratives. | Baghdad (Iraq)–History–2003-
Classification: LCC: KMJ110.O53 O53 2016 | DDC: 340.092/0567–dc23

Law and Rockets

An American Lawyer in Iraq

"And I have seen what other men sometimes have thought they've seen."

> Arthur Rimbaud, *Le Bateau Ivre* (The Drunken Boat), trans. Ted Berrigan

Introduction

I WAS ALREADY WORKING AS A young lawyer in Panama when I came across a copy of Norwood Allman's *Shanghai Lawyer* in a used bookstore in Minneapolis. Allman was an American lawyer who practiced before the United States District Court for China. The Imperial Japanese Army had invaded Shanghai and closed foreign institutions there. Allman avoided arrest and internment and made it back to the United States, where he wrote a book about his experiences working as an attorney in China.

When Allman published his book in 1942, the United States was at war against Japan. Allman fully expected that Chiang Kai-Shek would be restored to power and the foreign concessions in Shanghai renewed. The court where he had built his practice over many years would open again and he would return to the practice of law. He was wrong. Chiang's return to power was brief and the court simply disappeared. Allman never returned to China. In the United States he began a new career.

The closing of a court is a rare occurrence which most often happens on account of war. The courtrooms of the Venetian Republic host tour groups today; after Napoleon conquered the Republic in 1798 there was no use for them. In 1982 the United States District Court for the Canal Zone closed due to the Panama Canal Treaties. United States district courts rarely go out of business: The chief judge of the Fifth Circuit Court of Appeals, Charles Clark, attended the ceremony. So did a Panamanian colonel named Manuel Noriega, who did not wear a general's rank until later.

The Southern District of Florida in Miami has built four new "main" courthouses since 1983 on account of the drug war. Today, like the empty Venetian courts, one of those Miami courthouses is no longer needed. The drug war has been replaced with real wars.

Law is not normally thought of as an international profession; it travels poorly. British lawyers enjoy more of an international practice since they are welcome in those countries where the outline of the Empire's footprint can still be seen. Today, British-flavored courts and arbitration centers with common-law rules and procedures are growing up in places like Dubai and Qatar.

The American lawyer who wants to work overseas has been less fortunate. The public sector has a limited amount of foreign practice opportunities and the private sector is even more limited. Nevertheless, some Americans have practiced law internationally. Allman was one of them and I am fortunate to have been one of their number too. Allman left a record of his experiences practicing law overseas. I take my lead from him; I feel I have a duty to do the same.

After practicing for several years in Panama, I went north to Miami. South Florida was the epicenter of the War on Drugs, and if you were an attorney who had tried a few cases, spoke Spanish and had gone to high school in Colombia it was hard not to get involved. I had a drug war practice for several years. But with no enemy to surrender, no Reichstag to storm or embassy to evacuate by helicopter, the drug war just kind of petered out.

My next overseas mission was Saudi Arabia. I had been trying to get back to Latin America when I got the call. By 9/11 I was already in Riyadh. Before the airplanes hit the Twin Towers and the Pentagon, Saudi Arabia had been a faithful ally in the Cold War struggle against Communism. Saudis could pick up U.S. tourist visas at travel agencies—only exceptional cases merited an interview at the embassy. After 9/11 all of this changed and Saudi Arabia came to be seen as untrustworthy if not an outright enemy. My practice in Saudi Arabia was mainly corporate/commercial, consisting of contracts, construction matters and some dispute resolution.

I was not yet fifty years old when the United

States went to war against Iraq. Unlike the drug war, this was a real war. In March, 2003 I flew back to Saudi Arabia in an empty Lufthansa jet. Everyone who could was leaving the Gulf in anticipation of the war; virtually no one was traveling in the opposite direction. British Airways pulled out of the Kingdom entirely that March, 2003. Saddam had bombed Riyadh during the first Gulf War and people were afraid he would aim his Scud missiles at Riyadh once again.

At night on Saudi cable I watched Iraqi television. The Iraqi Army's press office had moved to an underground bunker. Whenever a bomb exploded closely, the newsroom curtains swayed back and forth prompting the uniformed telepresenters to hesitate—but just for a moment. Tariq Azziz, Saddam's press minister, tried to reassure the Iraqi public that all was well despite the American bombing raids. Herman Goering had once similarly reassured the German public that no bombs would ever fall on Berlin. Both were wrong.

Officially the war was over shortly after it began. The Iraqi Army put up little resistance to American forces, and the drive to Baghdad was more about moving men and equipment through the desert rather than an inch by inch fight for land. American troops reached Baghdad and quickly dismantled what was left of Iraqi command and control centers. They took out the Al-Jazeera news office in the Palestine Hotel with a rocket just for good measure. The embedded American media needed a photo op so one of the many statues of Saddam was pulled down with the cameras rolling. There had been little popular resistance to Saddam, but it wasn't difficult to find jubilant Iraqis who thought that if they pulled down one of Saddam's statues the Americans would go home.

Then George Bush declared "Mission Accomplished" on board an aircraft carrier and everyone thought, "that's that."

The French ambassador to Saudi Arabia knew that it wasn't. The ambassador, probably an intelligence officer, had accompanied the French foreign minister to a meeting with Dick Cheney in January, 2003, just before the invasion. The minister told Cheney, "Our governments agree to disagree on Iraq. Fine. But we know that you are going in and we know that you will win. So we want to help with the reconstruction; we want to help rebuild Iraq. What are the post-invasion plans?"

Cheney told him there weren't any. Looking back, it is simply incredible to think that there were no post-invasion plans but there were none.

Cheney and his team hadn't thought that far ahead. Their mission was to disarm Saddam Hussein; whatever happened afterwards simply wasn't their concern. This became painfully obvious when the looting started. American troops stood by while the National Museum in Baghdad was sacked. Their rules of engagement did not include any orders to protect Iraqi institutions. This would soon change.

The United States threw together an occupation government when it realized that under the rules and usages of war it was responsible for running the country. The Administration believed that just like in Panama, Germany and Japan the aftermath of invasion would primarily be political. Everyone thought that it would be so easy.

But it wasn't. Six years later the Americans are once again bogged down in a guerrilla war. Politics in Baghdad are divisive. Only a unity government could have sufficient moral authority to stop the fighting. The new Iraqi government was fiercely partisan and lacked power. Saddam was finally captured, tried in irregular Iraqi proceedings and then executed. The rule of law was mostly theater; the invading army was still in control. But the execution of the country's former leader was very, very real. Surely the execution would stop the fighting.

But it didn't. The fighting went on. But then General Petraeus' surge tactics showed some success. The tide was turning. In May, 2009 the Saudis finally listened to British Airways' years of begging and decided to let them resume flights to Riyadh. I was on their first flight out, returning to my house on 46th Street in Miami to work on the appeal of a murder case with tenuous links to the Obama White

House. The client, Tom Tuduj, was desperate: at sentencing his own lawyers said that they considered him their enemy. The learned judge nevertheless permitted the sentencing proceedings to continue.

The Miami I came back to was not the one I had left years before. They say you can't go home again for a reason. The most conservative American investment—the owner-occupied single family home—had lost 2/3rd's of its value in a severe economic recession. The U.S. Treasury's Troubled Assets Rescue Program (TARP) was sold to the American people as a solution for struggling homeowners, but the sale was a deception: as everyone knows today, TARP was a bank sector bail-out. I was so upside-down on the house that it made no sense to keep it. There really wasn't anything for me in Miami anymore. It was time to leave.

One day I received a telephone call from Liam Mooney, a recruiter who runs Blue Pencil Legal, a top-notch recruiting firm in Dubai. He told me about a German firm with offices in several cities in the Middle East. They even had an office in Baghdad. They were opening an office in the Green Zone. The firm is called MENA Associates, or MENA. They needed someone to staff that office.

MENA Associates is a law firm with offices throughout the Middle East: Cairo, Damascus, Dubai, Baghdad and Erbil, in Iraqi Kurdistan. Like not a few international firms, there was a link to the international firm Baker & McKenzie where the firm's principal. Florian Amereller, had once been an associate. Liam told me that the firm had a good reputation and was aggressively moving into Iraq. MENA appeared to be a medium-sized firm, small enough so that the individual is not overlooked, but large enough to be able to offer a full range of services to its clients.

I was reassured by the Baker & McKenzie connection; many firms claim to be international ones but in fact are not. The presence of several functioning offices meant that I would not be on my own, even though the Green Zone office was small. There is a real difference between small and large law firms when it comes to administrative support. What is routine in larger firms can be an event in smaller firms. Having grown out of a larger firm, MENA would surely be familiar with the importance of developed back-office support. Even though I had never worked for a German firm before, I did not anticipate any difficulties. I had grown up in what had been a German-settled farming town in Illinois and had recently worked closely with a German lawyer in Riyadh.

Then Liam asked me,

"Would you be interested in going to Iraq?"

I said yes. This is the story of my brief career as an attorney in Iraq.

Miami–Cairo

July 22, 2010

JULY 2010. A tropical storm without a name settled on Miami and soaked the city. It was five in the morning and my two oversize suitcases were in the back of the pickup truck getting soaked. I was moving to Iraq and taking too much with me. Before six a.m. there was still relative peace on the roads. There was little traffic between Midtown and the airport; a straight shot from the entrance ramp at Miami Avenue to and past LeJeune Road. Traffic was starting to build up in the other direction; by 7:30 it would already be bumper to bumper. Inside the airport was another story. Flights from Brazil and Argentina arrived at three and four in the morning; the terminal was full of vacationers seeking to escape the Southern hemisphere's winter.

Since I was going to Iraq I really didn't have any reason to keep a house in Miami. But I knew from past experience that selling a house is never a hands-off affair. There is a constant back and forth with the realtor, documents to be signed, questions that have to be answered.

I asked my friend Donna if she would help me to handle day to day property matters while I tried to sell my house. Donna is an unemployed astrologer, qualified paralegal and former girlfriend of of Tony Garrudo, one of the principals of the Willie Falcón and Sal Magluta speedboat smuggling operation. Willie and Sal were legends in South Florida and for years handled transportation for the Medellin cartel. With these qualifications she could easily handle any matter relating to my home in Miami. In exchange, I told her that she could sell the furniture and other items left in the house in a yard sale and keep the proceeds.

My son Max drove me to the airport. A porter helped me unload the suitcases for the flight to New York. My suitcases could not be checked all the way through to Cairo; the firm had not sent me a ticket for the connecting flight. This is what happens when you travel on multiple tickets. I slept a little on the airplane to prepare myself for the ordeal that would be JFK; somehow I would have to lug these suitcases by myself from one terminal to another. I had spent the previous two weeks lifting boxes and packing. Now I hoped that I would be able to manage all the weight alone. It was good to have Max along to help and sad to say good-bye. He is a twenty-year old undergraduate studying in Chicago and has a full schedule of responsibilities and activities.

July 22, 2010

At JFK there is a People Mover which carries passengers from terminal to terminal. With all of my luggage using the escalators was out of the question, but somehow I managed. Checking in at Egyptair was routine; Americans are given visas at the airport in Cairo. In 2002 an Egyptair flight from New York to Cairo crashed in the Atlantic. The National Transportation Safety Board concluded that the pilot had committed suicide. The Egyptian authorities reached a different conclusion. The Americans felt that the Egyptian's invocation of Allah in prayer was a sign of his lethal intentions. These cultural conclusions troubled me because I know that in Arabic God is invoked constantly.

Despite the accident, Egyptair remains a popular choice for travel to the Middle East because their fares are low. The general view is that an old accident is less important than low prices. In the Middle East, history is fickle. An Arab proverb says, "if it is not seen, it did not happen." Thus, passengers shouldn't be worried. Move along, please; here there is nothing for you to see.

The presence of a Coptic priest waiting in the gate area wearing an upside-down stubby stovepipe hat could only remind me of the need for spiritual protection of some kind. Next to the Triple 7 there was an Aer Lingus Airbus boarding as well. I couldn't see any priests at their gate. Perhaps religion is less of an issue on Aer Lingus flights.

As welcome as a vacation in Ireland would be, there would be no vacation for me. I was on my way to a war zone.

July 23

Cairo. Marriott Hotel in Zemalek. The flight was nine hours long. It wasn't too bad.

When I arrived in Cairo my suitcases were still damp from the Miami downpour. I unpacked them so they could dry out. I had received no instructions at all as to what to bring, so I had just guessed. I guessed wrong. Business suits may be the required uniform for attorneys in the United States but would be rarely used in the Green Zone. Black leather dress shoes would not only instantly be covered in dust but were not optimal for running. Slipping and falling during a mortar attack means that you won't reach the shelter. Still, if you fall, try to position your feet towards the direction of the blast so the shrapnel won't have your head as a target. And if there is only small arms fire, remember to crouch since ricocheting bullets hug the floor. Unfortunately no one provided me with necessary instructions like these. My mind was full of presumptions and guesses. Probably the biggest mistake I made was thinking that Iraq was safe.

Today I will meet Florian Amereller. On Monday, I should be leaving for Baghdad. There was a note that I would go via Abu Dhabi. This seems odd. A lot of things haven't been settled.

July 24

In the mid-afternoon Florian came to the hotel to pick me up. We went straight to the MENA office in Cairo where I met some of the attorneys working there. It seems to be a professional operation; it's a real office and not just a shop run by a sole practitioner. MENA's name is on the door. Once again I have an overseas job. Back in the saddle and all that. Just a couple of days ago I was hanging out on 46th Street; now I'm back in Big Law on my way to Baghdad.

Florian is married with children. He brought a Panamanian family to Egypt to help out at home. Arnulfo introduced me to the Panamanian family's old son, Arnulfo. Arnulfo has been in Egypt long enough to learn Arabic. Arnulfo tells me that he is excited about the office in Iraq and asks me question after question. I can't answer most of them as I have yet to be briefed. Arnulfo says that he doesn't think he will ever go to Iraq. As the conversation continues, it becomes obvious that Arnulfo has no real interest in Iraq whatsoever. The real reason for our conversation was to see if I could really speak and understand Spanish. Arnulfo was to report back with his findings to Florian. I know some Panamanian slang. *Chuleta*.

So, one of the first persons I met was an informant; a spy.

Florian is multi-tasking and not sure what to do with me. He has several overlapping dinner engagements. He is a busy man. He boasted that he billed clients for several hour's work on the days his children were born.He suggests that Arnulfo take me to see the pyramids. He assumed that they would be open. Around 7:00 p.m. we left his home.

The pyramids had been closed for two hours when we left. No traffic may enter after five p.m. By the time we arrived it was after 8:30 and pitch black. Perhaps Florian wasn't aware of this detail. I'll try to go tomorrow, but given the state of things I don't think I'll get a chance. Florian is keen that I get to the Green Zone right away.

July 25

I wake up at 7:45 a.m.; there is a text message for me: we are leaving for Dubai promptly at nine. There will be no return trip to the pyramids. I checked out of the hotel after rushing to repack the suitcases. Luckily, I accomplished everything on time. Florian wanted to drop by the office before going to the airport even though we didn't have much time. Traffic was bad; it was stressful.

July 25

Florian wanted to drop by the office before we went to the airport. At the office I met Killian Balthazar, a German M&A attorney. The Cairo office had a good deal of depth for a medium-size firm. This was good news.

After less than a half hour in the office we drove to the airport for a Singapore Airlines flight to Dubai. Singapore Airlines is part of the Star Alliance, which includes United Airlines. The cabin crew was very attentive. I figured I'd at least pick up some frequent flyer miles.

We arrived in Dubai and went to the Marriott Four Corners hotel on Sheikh Zayed Road near MENA's Dubai office. There was no time to check in. Florian wanted to go to the office immediately. We left our suitcases at the hotel. The office within walking distance, located just a few doors away in a building that fronted on Sheikh Zayed Road with a good view of the Dubai Metro.

I had a quick meet and greet with the attorneys and staff. Perhaps ten employees worked there. I found an empty office and waited for Florian. I thought that there might be personnel matters to attend to, but that wasn't the case. At some point after 5 p.m. we left the office and returned to the hotel so we could check in. Florian said we would be in Dubai for a few days so I started unpacking my suitcases.

In the evening, Florian and I went for dinner at

MJ's Steakhouse in the Alcazar Hotel a few doors down from our hotel. This was our first opportunity to speak at length. Florian is well-connected to the secret world of the Middle East, the real world behind the one that gets reported. He tells me that Arafat's finance minister was a Kurd who now lives in Egypt. Arafat was offered 98% of the borders, millions of dollars and for refugees, 400,000 visas for the United States and a proportional amount for Canada. But Arafat said "no."

I think I made a good decision by allying myself with what seems to be a quality firm. I wonder what awaits me in Iraq. I do not yet know what this new life will be like.

July 26

Florian is making preparations for Iraq. I feel that I'm already losing contact with people, but it's supposed to be that way.

Tomorrow the Green Zone and Baghdad.

In the evening Florian and I and a few of the Dubai-based attorneys went out for dinner. One of the attorneys complimented me on my bravery. Somehow this is not reassuring. Or perhaps I have simply turned a blind eye to the danger. For me, this started out not so much as a journey to what the Arabs call the "House of War," but merely as a return to the Middle East. I have never given much thought to the danger. But tomorrow I will land in Baghdad and in a very real sense begin a new life. I'm cutting off the life that I had before. Very little of it will survive. I have not thought about being brave. I simply have ignored whatever danger there might be.

I asked around today about what I should expect in Iraq and no one could tell me anything. No one but Florian had gone to the Green Zone. There was no briefing, no orientation, no plans: I just need to get there. There has been no coordination with the military authorities. I should just go.

Green Zone

July 27

I GOT UP EARLY again to make our mid-morning flight to Baghdad. I marched the platoon of suitcases downstairs, Florian had already approached a group of a taxi drivers who were milling about in front of the hotel. He asked which of them really knew the way to the airport in Abu Dhabi, which was an hour away. Apparently Florian had once had difficulties with a driver who really did not know how to get to the airport, though there is just one road to follow. The drivers initially all claimed familiarity with the route, but then started correcting each other. Eventually, one of the drivers convinced Florian that he knew the way. It was a struggle getting my luggage into the taxi. Florian had only one suitcase that was just a little too large to check in if you were flying economy class, but you might get away bringing it aboard if you were flying business class. Florian wasn't staying in the Green Zone for long anyway, but I didn't know that. The trunk finally closed on my bags and we were off headed down Sheikh Zayed Road to

Abu Dhabi, Dubai's wealthier but less flashy sibling. There wasn't much traffic and soon we reached the airport turn-off from the main road.

We were flying Etihad business class from Terminal 1 and the separate check-in counter for Baghdad made the fact of our destination all too real. There were a few Iraqis already in line when we arrived. Though we were flying business class, because of security you can only have one carry-on; this is strictly enforced. Florian's bag had to be checked. The plane used for the flight was a small Airbus, the A320. The plane was brand-new, like most of Etihad's fleet.

In the business class lounge a German government official, Dr. Hans von Traven, greeted Florian and the two of them discussed plans in German. Dr. Hans is an academic. We discussed the current situation in Iraq. He disagreed with Florian's optimism and told me it would be ten years before things settled down in Iraq. He compared the current situation to that of Germany after the war.

As you are landing in Baghdad, depending on which side of the aircraft you are sitting, you can see a vast palace on an island in a lake. There is a construction crane visible from the air. I never learned whether this was one of Saddam's palaces or not. From the vantage point of the flight path there are no obvious signs of war, no signs of bombing. No bomb craters are visible.

The jetways at the newly-named Baghdad International Airport are not used. There were one or two planes parked next to the terminal but the other planes—and there weren't many—are on the tarmac nearby. Some of them had been sitting for a long time. During the sanctions period prior to the invasion obtaining spare parts was difficult. A lawsuit against the Iraqi government resulted in a judgment and the seizure of aircraft. Rather than risking the seizure of aircraft by creditors, it was safer to let them sit. Only our plane and a Royal Jordanian B-737 were in use.

After arrival, the ramp crew rolled up stairs to the front of the aircraft. We disembarked to a bus which we rode from the plane to the terminal. Arriving passengers quickly line up under signs that say, "Iraqi" or "Other." If you do not have a resident's visa, you move to a counter on the left side of the Arrivals Hall where an Iraqi immigration officer asks for your passport and then disappears into a back room. After a while the immigration officer returns to invite you in. I entered the room and was met with a military officer who asked me, "USA?" There were no other questions. Military members do not need visas. Apparently I successfully passed the interview, so I was asked to wait outside.

After an interminable wait my passport was returned by the immigration officer with a full-passport-page visa glued to one of the pages. There is no picture on the visa. The cost of the visa was only $2. Some countries charge much more for visas on arrival; in others, visas on arrival are not available at all. I returned to the "Other" line where my passport was stamped yet again.

Inside the airport multiple signs warn against smoking in the terminal. Somehow the risk of second-hand smoke pales when compared to other more obvious risks. With so many other ways to lose your life, it's reassuring that at least someone takes the long view.

Despite the visa-related delay, by the time I made it though Immigration not a single bag had arrived on the carousel. It would take another half hour before the bags started appearing. Customs was just a smile.

Up to this point we have seen no American military personnel.

Two men met us at the airport. One of the men was Ahmed Al-Marid, a lawyer working with the firm. Ahmed would be working with me in the Green Zone. Though Ahmed had proper credentials to enter the Green Zone, the other man, Yaser Al-Ani, did not. Since Yaser did not have the proper credentials to enter the Zone, Florian had arranged for a security detail from Sabre Security to bring us into the Zone. It was less expensive for them to bring us in after we had reached the perimeter rather than going all the way out to the airport. We walked to the parking lot and got in Ahmed's SUV. Near the airport, we stopped for gas at a base held jointly by U.S. and Iraqi forces. The gas station had a small PX and souvenir shops. Gas is $4 per gallon. The shops, I am told, are controlled by a well-connected Kurd.

The East-West road between Baghdad and the airport has been named "Route Irish" by Coalition forces. As we continued towards the city, we quickly ran into a checkpoint run by the Iraqi Army. We passed through routinely, without incident. It's not clear what the term "Iraqi forces" means given that the Iraqi Army was disbanded and the entire country is under U.S. military command. There is a civilian government but that government only has that power permitted by the commanders in Washington. After a while, I noticed that there were concrete walls on both side of the highway. The walls separated the highway from the Aymal neighborhood, a stronghold for al-Qaeda. American troops never go there. As an American you can go in, but you won't come out.

The ubiquitous checkpoints present a more immediate risk. At the next checkpoint U.S. troops were standing in front of a sign announcing that the use of deadly force is authorized. This is nothing like a DUI checkpoint in the U.S.: this is much, much worse. Vehicles have been shot at and people killed while going through checkpoints. Our security guard driver cautions me not to make any sudden movements. Despite the warning, I was able to get a photograph of an armored personnel carrier as it was leaving the area.

We continued our drive along Route Irish into town. At intervals there are steel and wooden watchtowers on scaffolding some fifty feet high. The watchtowers are accessed by staircases. These staircases are covered with canvas so that no one can see troops going up or coming down the stairs; if they are seen they will be shot at.

At one point we had to stop for an American military convoy crossing the road. I tried to take a picture but everyone in the car shouted at me to put the camera away. Pointing anything in the direction of the convoy was a threat. American troops, they said, were known to fire at the least provocation. I was sternly warned by Ahmed who was experienced in proper checkpoint behavior. A camera could easily be mistaken for a gun and might invite a deadly response.

We continued on and came to a bridge. Proper identification is necessary to enter the bridge because the bridge leads to the Green Zone. We show passports and ID cards and they let us pass. The bridge is deserted; no traffic crosses it except for us.

In military terms, a loaded weapon is said to be in a "red" state; an unloaded weapon, "green." The Green Zone is a place where weapons do not have to be chambered, it is a place where weapons are unloaded. For that reason it is not entirely safe. If an enemy succeeds in making it past the checkpoints they will initially face little resistance. There is a false sense of safety because of this. If an infiltrator succeeds in bringing a weapon into the Green Zone he can do a lot of damage before soldiers can load their weapons. This has already happened in the Green Zone; I am told that it happens frequently in Afghanistan. The Green Zone was more or less safe, but you were exposed to fire all the way to the airport.

After clearing the bridge we pulled over and stopped underneath an overpass where we change into a vehicle sent by Sabre Security. Sabre operates both the barracks where I will be staying and the business center where MENA's office is located. Yasir moved to the driver's side and left with Ahmed's car. Sabre has sent two vehicles for us. The windows in the cars that took us into the Green Zone didn't work. The new car is a "hard" car, a Mercedes with B6 shielding. This provides adequate shielding against automatic weapons fire, but is ineffective against roadside bombs. Nothing protects against roadside bombs. They call these landmines "improvised explosive devices" or IED's. Calling them improvised suggests that the danger they represent is haphazard. This is a mistake. They are an effective weapon manufactured by an irregular army. Against them there is only the defense of speed, luck and hope of malfunction. At least we are not in a "soft" car. A soft car has no shielding at all, leaving you vulnerable. The new vehicle seemed slower and the windows wouldn't roll down. The air conditioning wasn't strong enough to keep up with Baghdad's rising thermometer. In the summer it can reach 120 degrees Fahrenheit (50° C).

We passed a third checkpoint and enter the Green Zone. We cut to the right and drive along a blast wall. The blast wall is fifteen feet high and cuts the two lane road down to one lane for all traffic. This turns this potion of the road system into a giant one-way maze. Oncoming drivers have to share the roadway. Fortunately there is little traffic.

The area had been a suburb built for Saddam Hussein's top army and government officials. It had been trashed in the invasion but was slowly being rebuilt. The paved road ends and we continued on, stirring up clouds of dust. We can no longer see the second convoy car trailing us. It is not clear why the road is no longer paved. Perhaps it was paved once; perhaps a bomb is the reason why the concrete is missing. We are in an area that was once the center of Saddam's power. Corrugated metal surrounds what were once villas and turns them into compounds.

The Sabre Compound is in District 215, Street 7, House 2. Sabre built improvised housing using empty shipping containers stacked in the front and back yards of a former Iraqi Army general's villa. Military-style barracks have been added that look like junior officer's quarters. Those that guard us endure less pleasant accommodations. They live in the 20 foot shipping containers that have been converted into living quarters.

We leave the hardened car and enter the main gate. We show identification and are allowed access to the compound. My suitcases were unloaded at the patio just inside the Sabre Security headquarters. There are small tables and chairs out in the open on a concrete floor. Four white porcelain sinks stand out in the open, supplied with bacterial soap dispensers and paper towels. Why is there a need for so prominent a sanitation feature? These are not sinks for Muslim ablutions; they are to keep away germs. Is there such a risk of disease here?

There is an asphalt sidewalk a few feet from the building's edge separating the barracks and the rest of the compound from the outer blast wall. There is no way to tell what is on the other side of the wall without climbing the corrugated metal stairs to the second story of stacked shipping containers. The staircase, with one cutback, leads to another door. Through this door are the offices of the companies that have arrived to do business in the new Iraq: Petronas, from Malaysia. Statol, from Norway. Korea Gas. And us.

July 27

Down the stairs you turn right back onto the sidewalk. There is a wooden door with an unlocked combination lock. Pushing it open leads to a long, tiled corridor. The building is made of cinderblock. There are rooms on each side of the corridor. I am shown one of them. This one is to be mine. There is a free standing closet, a single bed, a desk and chair. On the wall there is a 21 inch LCD screen. There was a small shower in the adjoining bathroom. It was large enough to stand in, but not large enough to turn around in. Worse, water coming out of the tap was cold. Getting hot water should not have been a problem where the temperatures approached 50 C, but it was. Perhaps the waterlines ran through air conditioned rooms. In the absence of hot water, you had to turn the water on to wet yourself. Then you would turn the water off, lather up, and then turn the water on again to rinse off. This is called a Navy shower and not only does it conserve water, but it keeps your time under the cold water to a minimum. This was a difficulty I had not considered in coming to Iraq.

Florian asked me, "what do you think?" I said, "Petersburg FCI." I realize that he has no idea what I am talking about. Petersburg, Virginia is home to a federal prison. I used to visit clients there. The decor was similar. Then it occurs to me that he is afraid I'll say, fuck this, and in a state of fear run away screaming. But how can I scream?

I've just been introduced to my new home.

After being shown my new quarters, I was taken immediately to a security briefing at Sabre's operation center. The center looks like it is equipped to monitor space shuttle launches. There is a large, theater-sized telescreen filling a wall. Elevated rows lead up to back wall; there are tables running from one end of the room to the other; computer monitors are on top of many. The screen shows a map of Baghdad, it is lit up with colored markers showing the location of reported incidents; text scrolls rapidly across the bottom of the screen with the latest news.

Tony Devlin, the Ops manager, stood in front of the screen and began the briefing for my benefit.

There are two to three rocket attacks per month. I should expect the pace of the attacks to continue for the time being. The target is the U.S. Embassy. Unfortunately, Sabre Security is just to the northeast of the Embassy, perhaps 2-3 kilometers away. The mortars and rockets the insurgents use are not that accurate; they have only rudimentary targeting systems. A one degree mistake in aiming a mortar can have deadly consequences.

I learned a new acronym: "PPE," for "personal protective equipment." My PPE consists of a helmet and a matching bullet-resistant flak jacket. The PPE was kept in a closet in each room. I was instructed on what to do in a case of a rocket attack. High-pitched sirens will sound before the rockets arrive. I was told that it was important to put on the equipment whenever there was a warning siren and to lie on the floor in my quarters or wherever I found myself when the sirens went off. The "all clear" sounds like a two-tone European police siren.

After the briefing Florian wanted to go to a commercial area that was behind the football practice field in front of the compound. I asked him what was the purpose of the strange inverted-U shaped concrete structures on the side of the field.

"They're bomb shelters. When you hear the siren, you run inside and wait."

Since the shelters were not enclosed, they didn't seem particularly safe. Yet I suppose they were better than nothing. We continued walking to find one or two small shops. There was a convenience store locally known as the "Sugar Shack." Nearby was a door which opened into a large warehouse. The warehouse was not just a liquor store, it was a liquor storage facility. A motherload of alcohol. There were hundreds of cases stacked nearly to the ceiling. Every type of alcoholic beverage was available. I learned later that this warehouse was off-limits to military personnel.

Under General Order No. 1, the U.S. government made an effort to respect Iraqi laws and traditions. Even though alcohol was banned in Iraq, the U.S. military was dry. Unlike in other countries, to avoid criticism the U.S. forces did not set up saloons or bars where drinks could be had. A substantial amount of booze had been requisitioned for the thirsty soldiers, but unfortunately General Order No. 1 made the warehouse liquor store off-limits and prohibited soldiers from drinking—at least officially. Florian purchased a few bottles, including one or two of Iraqi manufacture. Then we headed back to the compound.

That evening I heard the sirens for the first time. When you hear them you are supposed to drop to the floor and wait for the all clear. There was a rocket attack that first evening. First came a series of multi-colored flares. I was outside eating with my colleagues when the warning sirens went off. No one dropped a fork or dropped to the floor. Their only accommodation to the war was to halt the conversation since it is impossible to talk over a rocket warning siren.

Within fifteen minutes or so, several unlit helicopters flew overhead from the north heading towards the flares. The helicopters were completely dark—there were no display lights whatsoever, only their black fuselages against the Baghdadi night sky.

My quarters are similar to a college dormitory or a federal prison. The similarity must not be solely a coincidence. Like in prison, I don't have to pay for my meals, except in some psychological sense. Supposedly, there is regular mail service, though I never saw a letter until I involved myself in the postal system. The Sabre Security compound is a self-contained unit. There is a laundry, kitchen, rec room, security theater and a gym. There is even a bar. Unlike the warehouse, this bar was not off-limits and so U.S. military personnel who had a reason to visit Sabre could take advantage of the facilities.

What is the line from *Apocalypse Now*? When Robert Duvall forces Lance the surfer to ride the waves amidst incoming rocket fire? Martin Sheen's voice-over said, "the more they tried to imitate home the further away it was."

The streets around the compound are a mess. There has been no real reconstruction following the bombings and the general invasion. The Sabre compound started with a single villa and grew by accretion. Despite the billions in aid sent, the streets in the Green Zone are still poorly paved, full of craters and holes made during the conflict and yet unrepaired.

This is the frontier. If you have been to prison you know that you need very little to live. When I arrived in Baghdad I was surprised how quickly I tolerated the accommodations, a cell in a protected compound in the Green Zone. I sit in Baghdad behind the walls of a compound with walls like a prison.

The Legal Environment

IN DEALING WITH LEGAL problems, often one of the most difficult tasks is determining what the law is. Getting a clear answer from a lawyer is not an easy task. Complicate matters with a different terrain, culture and legal system is a guarantee that clear answers will remain elusive. I started researching Iraqi law before I left the United States. When I arrived in Iraq, I continued the effort.

Iraq's legal traditions are ancient and begin with the work of Hammurabi the Lawgiver. Islam brought the *shari'a*, a word meaning "path" in Arabic. Islamic law became the law of the land. In the 20th century Iraq modernized its legal system, enacting a civil code in 1953 which was in large part based on the Egyptian Civil Code. The Egyptian code was based on European systems which trace their roots to Roman law. In 1958 Iraqi army officers overthrew the Hashemite king. In 1968, Saddam Hussein took control and insisted on the state's right to intervene in legal affairs. Though a new constitution was passed in 1970, eventually Saddam ruled by decree. The state intervened in order to correct errant judicial decisions. The judiciary was very much a part of the regime.

With the fall of Saddam, the Coalition Provisional Authority began administering the country. Starting in April, 2003, the CPA issued orders which "suspended or replaced" Iraqi laws. The idea was to modernize Iraqi laws in order to support Iraq's economic development.

CPA Order No.17 granted immunity to defense contractors from jurisdiction. This was a controversial provision which led to friction. The United States has been sensitive about exposing its troops to the courts of another country, and sometimes even its own. On June 28, 2004 the CPA was abolished and its powers transferred to the Iraqi government. The new government enacted a constitution in October, 2005. Existing laws continue to be valid under the new constitution, even those enacted by the CPA. Many CPA orders remained in place, though some have been superseded by new Iraqi laws. A Status of Forces agreement was signed in 2009 and the contractors lost their immunity, but U.S. troops continue to be outside Iraqi law. Meanwhile, the war continued.

There are two CPA orders which remain in place that are important for Iraq's legal and business environment. The CPA created an agency to monitor public corruption. The Iraqi constitution continued that agency' work. The Banking Law, CPA Order No. 94, Annex A, remains in force and is referred to by post-constitution Iraqi legislation.

Many sources of law constitute the legal environment in Iraq. The shifting legal environment means that government officials are often unaware of which laws to apply. Determining the law to apply is an exercise in feeling your way.

The Office

July 28

FLORIAN STAYED ONLY one day. In retrospect, it wasn't clear why he had come at all. He left early in the morning. Left on my own, I hit the ground running.

The office is on the second floor, upstairs from my room. Several companies maintain offices on the second floor, including Statol from Norway and Petronas from Malaysia. In addition to the multinationals, there is a local insurance brokerage, Iraqgate Insurance, the only foreign-owned insurance company in the country. The office door has an electronic lock which can only be unlocked by entering a key code. The system is mechanical in case power is lost.

In addition to rooms housing the branch offices of several multinational companies, upstairs was also the business office for Sabre itself. Sabre handled not only personal security, but arranged for visas and was experimenting with sponsoring corporate formations. In addition to sales and billing, the liaison team worked with the American authorities to obtain certain classes of credentials for Sabre visitors and residents. They also coordinated reservations for the available rooms they had on the compound. Personnel matters involving the Nepalese and Ugandan soldiers who worked for Sabre were also handled from the business office. There were about eight people working at cubicles with just enough room for them all. The employees were of different nationalities. There were Australians, South Africans and one or two Iraqi's. But no Americans.

The office was empty save for two glass tabletops on saw horses. The tops could easily be removed. There were no books, no computers or printers. There was a whiteboard with nothing written on it. There was a telephone without any wires. This was the office.

There was no waiting room or reception. Because the office was small, anyone who walked in had to be dealt with immediately—by me. Whatever I was working on would have to stop.

There was a surprisingly strong Internet connection. But there were intermittent issues with both the Internet and the telephone line. A few days later Ahmed showed up with a SIM card for the office telephone. That is why, he explained, it's not working. It did not occur to me that the office phone would run on the same network as mobile phones. The reason is because the war and vandalism destroyed the wiring in the Green Zone. With the physical wires of POTS (plain old telephone service) unreliable or gone, the only way to get service was to make the jump to mobile.

Mobile phones can be used as triggering devices for IED's, roadside bombs. Military and security vehicles have long antennas on a boom that stretch out in front of the vehicle to jam cellphone signals. The jammers are powerful, so when one of them went by the phone in the office, running on the same mobile network, would go down. The Internet would go down, too. There was nothing you could do about it. You would be talking to someone in Europe or wherever and all of a sudden the phone line would drop. It was better to rely on e-mail.

There was no printer in the office. Next door, Sabre has set up a graphics department. They have a printer which I can use. I like to print things out—it is very difficult to proofread documents on the screen at low resolution. At higher resolution it is easier to catch errors, but no matter what you do it seems some always make it through. At MENA Associates, a typo was cause for crisis. I would soon learn it was that kind of place.

The young Iraqi guys who work in the graphics branch are wary of me and read everything that comes out of the printer. They know that I'm American—even though I haven't told them anything—and seem bewildered by my knowledge of Arab customs and practices. During a long conversation at lunch I quoted a hadith and they were astonished.

The IT guy is named Lum. He's in his 20's and from Kosovo. He's happy with the World Court decision confirming Kosovo's status as a republic. Everyone here is a soldier or related in some way to defense. I need to make friends with him. In the Middle East, IT and secretarial support are too often "unavailable." Before I arrived in Baghdad I asked for POP/SMTP mail settings so that I could start using my company e-mail address. Instead, they brought in a technician who took my laptop and returned it with the necessary settings already installed. While this is convenient, I knew that I was likely to be my own IT department in Baghdad. Because I didn't have the settings, in Baghdad I was on my own. Secretarial assistance? Nope. There are secretaries in Munich and Dubai, all busy with their own work and any assignment from Baghdad would be addressed when it gets addressed, thank you very much.

I hired my own virtual secretary, a paralegal in Florida who had taken some time off but was looking to get back into the workforce. Out of my own pocket, of course.

The Amereller firm had put together a legal guide to Iraq. Florian wanted to come out with a new edition and so he asked me to edit the guide. Previous revisions had not been made by native speakers and there was a need for extensive rewrites and changes. Still, the firm's guide was and remains a solid introduction to Iraqi law and practice.

Additionally, I was assigned the correction of a fifteen page Iraqi tax memo. It took me all day to confirm the legal points. Ahmed was unavailable to assist—he hadn't come into the office yet.

The cafeteria was filled with ten or so tables two meters long with chairs on either side. Six people could fit comfortably at a time. On the wall there was a 48" LCD screen which was always tuned to either the BBC or Al Jazeera news. The news always accompanied each meal, there was no other programming allowed.

Today at lunch and dinner I spilled my food tray. Both times. Immediately behind the exit door are sheets of heavy plastic strips to keep in the cool air; you often see these going into an air-conditioned warehouse. It is hard to navigate both the strips and the door. Until someone showed me how to go in and out. What I didn't realize is that you have to back out the door. That way the strips won't fall and hit your tray. Of course, if you do this it is impossible to tell what is on the other side of the door as you leave the facility. You won't see them coming if you have to walk through doors backwards. In a way, this is comforting.

A parent sending a child to summer camp will be given a list of what to bring as well as what to leave behind. I was given no such list; so I had to guess. Florian didn't have much to say about the situation on the ground in Iraq. He assumed that I knew. I had been on military bases before so I planned accordingly. I would have to take formal clothes because a lawyer must dress to look like a lawyer. The clients expect it and will be concerned if their lawyer does not look like a lawyer. The great legal historian Frederic Maitland wrote "a lawyer must be conventional lest he be no lawyer." It would be difficult to be conventional in the Green Zone, but at least I would look the part.

I shipped a few essential books and prepared additional boxes to be sent on later once I had become familiar with the territory. Later, I decided not to send for them. There was hardly enough room for them in either my quarters or the office. Personal effects were a luxury.

My suitcases went on top of the closet in my room, for the most part, filled with useless clothes that I couldn't wear. A pair of boots would have been helpful, but I couldn't find any place in-theater where they were sold.

Though I was supposed to be working with Ahmed, he hadn't yet come to the office. I had no idea where he was. I made a list of what was needed for the office and my room, in no particular order:

3-pronged plugs	*Official Gazette*
table lamp	night light
coffee maker	tub stopper
office phone	calendar
computer mouse	business cards
list of embassies	office stationery
legal pads	letterhead
air freshener	batteries
mail	

Dealing effectively with stateside problems is simply not possible from a war zone. As a rule, American systems are not set up to deal with international business and it is assumed that everything overseas works the same as it does back home. But they do not. Customs and practices overseas are far from the American norm. Services that are taken for granted back home are either difficult to access or simply don't exist. This is one of the most difficult aspects of being away.

E-mails bring distractions from home. It is impossible to deal with the realtor concerning the house on 46th Street; no, I can't just get a document notarized; no, it will be days for you to get mail from me. If you can't use e-mail or fax I can't help you. People don't realize how far away I really am. People ignore the fact that this is a war zone; the Iraq war is old news.

To move around freely in the Green Zone I have to apply for badges. Sabre Ops will handle the paperwork. Until the political situation stabilizes—

they are saying three months but I think five years is more likely—they say I can't go into the city safely without an armed escort.

I don't yet have an Iraqi telephone number. I've gone along making lists of what needs to be done in the office, of what I think is important. The office phone is a mobile—desk office telephones use SIM cards just like mobile, or cell phones. Because of the Coalition bombing wired telephones became unreliable. Poles came down and wiring was stolen. I saw a junction box near the football field that was empty, its doors left wide open to show that there was nothing left to steal.

The problem with office-based mobile phones is that electronic countermeasures interrupt cell phone signals. It doesn't matter if the cell phone is buried on the side of a road attached to a bomb or sitting on a desk. If a convoy goes by with ECM activated, your telephone call is over until the convoy passes and service is restored.

The clothes that I brought with me for the most part are unsuitable. Attorneys do not wear suits. For one, it is too hot. And dusty. A tie was my sole badge of professional status. My suits remained in the suitcase.

Today Jacob Leu, a Deputy Secretary of State, stated that American civilians living in Iraq will face security challenges once American troops leave. Duh. Supposedly the war will be declared 'over' by the end of next month and all American troops are supposed to leave by the end of 2011.

Meanwhile, the Iraqis hate us for upending their country. People stop speaking if I walk into a room even if they are speaking Arabic. They don't know how much I can understand.

Outside my window there is a blast wall. We are cut off from the outside.

There is a bright side to my living conditions. I have no commute, no gas expenses, no need for a car. All of a sudden my expenses have dropped to zero. In this light, being bothered once and a while with Miami problems isn't so bad.

My life has changed drastically. Do I even realize it?

July 30

Today is Max's birthday. I sent him an e-mail and will try to call him.

Last night there were two rocket attack warnings. For the first, I followed the instructions I have been given to lie on the floor though I did not put on the personal protective equipment. The second time, I did nothing.

I watched *Der Untergang* ("Downfall") on video. Someone it seemed appropriate. I also wrote to a friend in the U.S. and described the circumstances of my arrival.

With nothing else to do and being confined to the Green Zone, I spent my day off in the office. I am not the only one to do this.

More e-mails from America about the house. They just don't get it. I honestly don't have time for this.

Even though I am selling the house in Miami, there is an issue concerning property valuation after the real estate crash and my right to a Florida homestead exemption. The hearing before the Value Adjustment Board has finally been scheduled. For August 24. Wonderful. Because I am a civilian I do not get the benefits of the Soldiers and Sailors Relief Act. The law is designed to prevent litigation from going forward when one of the parties is in a war zone. You can't deal with war and litigation back home at the same time. But if you're a civilian, tough luck. The war doesn't matter. The scheduling of legal proceedings will go forward. This is another hidden tax that overseas Americans pay.

Tonight was the first night I heard a rocket explosion. It hit around 2230 or so. I was back in the office. A minute or so later, after the horse had left the barn, the warning siren sounded.

It occurs to me that because of all of the reckless things my countrymen have done here it will be impossible to live in Baghdad outside the Green Zone. It will be five years—or more—before the situation stabilizes. Do I want to live the next five years like this?

I spoke to Max and he so wanted to talk. I hope he understands that I am here so that I can make his life better. I owe that to him, at least.

I need a plan and can't let these things get me down.

Tomorrow I will work harder and accomplish more, rocket attacks or not.

July 31

I expected that the Green Zone would be more developed but it's not. Instead, it's a fortified slum. There is little commerce outside the military bases and these have been thrown together. Forward Operating Base (FOB) Prosperity sits on the grounds of one of Saddam's residences, known as As-Salam Palace. The main building is huge, with at least two hundred rooms and comprising over a million square feet of floorspace.

The palace itself was bombed out in the invasion. That was seven years ago. After the bombing, the building was not structurally safe. Rather than make repairs, they simply put up a chain link fence and declared the building off-limits. Now you can see the pigeons flying through what were once walls and windows. Pigeons now fly through what were once walls and windows. The excuse is that repairs can't be made with mortar fire coming in every night. So the building sits slowly crumbling, one of many architectural casualties of the invasion.

A two day weekend in the Islamic world is a great luxury. On the Saudi Arabian mothership the weekend is only a day and a half. In the Green Zone I was at the office on both days, that is, upstairs. Friday is the beginning of the weekend but it's a business day in Europe. So the office has to be manned; it can't be closed. Work is disorganized; I'm using a small netbook for everything and that isn't easy at all. There is no evidence of daily contributions from Ahmed—he's still nowhere to be found.

It's 00:30 and there haven't been any sirens yet. Tonight the insurgents are enjoying their weekend as well.

Precedents

IT WASN'T THAT LONG ago that lawyers were perfectly happy to work in a world with typewriters and books. When you opened law office, a West Publishing company salesman would call and try to sell you at least 400 books to populate your office law library. "You don't have to worry about the older stuff," was the advice he reassuringly gave, but "forget about old law" was somehow missing from the law school curriculum.

You did need to subscribe to the advance sheets, and these came out at least monthly and sometimes more often. Today's law would be superseded by tomorrow's. Building a library was much easier in civil law jurisdictions because you needed fewer books. In a civil law jurisdiction like Germany or France, you were prepared with just the codes: civil, commercial, procedural and perhaps criminal. The complete set would easily fit on a corner of the desk.

Computer-assisted legal research in the mid-90's was a luxury, but now it is a necessity. Before the mid-90's, legal resources on the growing Internet were spotty. The dedicated services like Lexis/Nexis and Westlaw were reliable and comprehensive. There were few competitors. West, a private company, sold itself when competitors started to appear. After all, judicial decisions were public documents, paid for by the public. West was just a repackager, albeit an extremely competent one, of material already in the public domain. Soon there was enough material on the Internet to replace the 400 books the West salesman wanted to earn a commission on. And then you didn't need books at all.

Things are different in the Middle East. Saudi Arabia has a six or seven volume compilation of its laws. If you need more than that, you have to visit the ministries. There you might find the information you need. Or you might not.

Fortunately, Iraq was in a different situation. Because of the invasion, the United Nations undertook a project to translate or collect translations of all Iraqi laws. The project was successful and the collection comprehensive. The United Nations did an excellent job of translating older Iraqi laws into English and maintaining a database of those laws. The UN put the collection on the Internet so obtaining copies of older Iraqi laws was possible. It was a simple matter to look up an Iraqi law on a subject and then see if there was a Coalition law on point.

However, it is one thing to have access to a collection and another to have the particular document ready to be read or printed out on your local computer. Research and downloading were required in all cases. This had to be done by me, while wearing the hat of all-purpose law clerk and legal researcher. Considering that we were supposed to have another office in the Red Zone, it was odd that the other resident Red Zone lawyers were mysteriously ensconced in an unvisitable office with apparently no legal resources whatsoever and no inclination to help or even visit their new colleague in the Green Zone.

As in Saudi Arabia, sometimes the only real way to be sure of current practice was to visit the ministry concerned, in person, and ask them what they were doing. The ministry may well have been asked the precise question before, and if they had they may have issued a ministerial instruction on the issue. If not, they could provide informal advice as to how they were treating this matter or that. IRS Letter Rulings and Ministerial Instructions are very much alike.

Visiting the ministries was Ahmed's job. The problem was that Ahmed was almost never around. He worked nights. Whenever he worked he did a good job, but his presence at the office was an event. So when Florian or a client would call asking for a legal opinion, or wanting to know who was the incumbent currently exercising an admittedly civilian function of the once all-powerful Revolutionary Guard, I would sometimes have to answer, "I don't know." Though that answer was correct, it was never the right one.

To make things worse, there were almost no legal precedents in the office. The term "precedents" needs an explanation. American lawyers are familiar with only one of the definitions of the legal term "precedents." They understand this word to mean the collection of prior judicial decisions that are published by courts and that must be followed. The other definition refers to the intellectual property of the firm itself; the forms and documents created or collected throughout the existence of the firm that can applied to new matters. These precedents are extremely valuable and distinguish large and old firms from small or new ones. Armed with an extensive precedent library, even a small firm can handle major matters.

Years later, when the Dewey, LeBoeuf firm ceased operations, I contacted the bankruptcy trustee to inquire about licensing the firm's precedents for use by another firm. According to the bankruptcy trustee, the Dewey "forms library" constituted protected attorney-client work product and had no commercial value. This is nonsense. What separates "Big Law" from small firms are forms libraries. With a decent forms library you don't have to reinvent the wheel or rush to the library every time there's a client inquiry.

We didn't have any kind of precedents library in the Green Zone. It was all greenfield, new. Perhaps there were precedents in Germany, Cairo, or Dubai, but I had access to no library. At least there would have been a law library in Miami. In Iraq I had to build my own. My colleagues in the Red Zone weren't sharing what they had, if they even existed.

Fortunately, I had my own precedents library which I had collected over the years. I was able to use many of my own documents because an international law practice is essentially a business practice and the problems are recurring ones. Few are truly new. There may be different fact patterns, but the underlying issue has been seen before. A sales representative failed to meet targets. A new sales director feels that the local agent isn't aggressive enough. A joint venture promises new opportunities. Someone has failed to pay a bill.

Legal problems can often be reduced to a formula: someone has failed to do something they were supposed to do.

I had brought a HP210 netbook and an iPad with me. Ahmed promised to bring a laptop soon. I felt I needed a typewriter. They are antiques but still useful. I always had one in the law offices where I had worked and there was no reason to let war change this practice. I found an "Empire" portable model on E-bay which was designed specifically for travel. The Seller in the UK checked with Federal Express and confirmed that they could deliver to the Green Zone.

In describing the work of an international lawyer in Shanghai in the 1930's, Norwood Allman wrote:

> "It was taken for granted that the American lawyer in Shanghai knew something about international law, maritime law, the laws of the District of Columbia, the decisions of the federal courts, equity, and the laws of most of the forty-eight of these United States. Cases in the American court frequently turned about the law of any one of the states, not to mention the laws of the Philippine Islands."
>
> Norwood F. Allman, *Shanghai Lawyer* (New York: Whittlesey House, 1943), 115–116.

Practicing in Iraq wouldn't be all that different.

There was nothing left to do but start assembling a working library of Iraqi laws and precedents.

Initial Matters

IN THE BEGINNING, the legal matters I handled had little to do with Iraq. Because of my Saudi legal experience Florian asked me to handle several matters involving that and other countries. I didn't have to be under fire in the Green Zone to handle these matters. I could have handled them from Dubai, Cairo or Germany, but somehow relocating never came up. So I handled them from the Green Zone.

One matter involved a German company that wanted to restructure its business in Saudi Arabia. From a business point of view this was fairly straightforward, but the problem is that Saudi Arabia welcomes certain kinds of businesses and discourages others. Wholesale and retail trading are particularly discouraged. Contractors will have a difficult road to travel to obtain proper licenses. Manufacturers willing to employ hundreds of local nationals will see only the red carpet. For others, it's not so easy.

In addition to the official local practice there are local customs and procedures to be navigated. In fairness, every country's legal system is like this. Conduct that is mandatory in one jurisdiction is punished in another. Send a letter to a federal judge in Miami and you risk contempt of court, or just a warning if you are a new attorney. File a motion instead of a letter in a federal case in New Jersey and the judge will ask why you did not send a letter like all the other attorneys. There are more than 3,000 counties in the United States so legal procedures end up being wildly diverse. Sometimes the lack of uniformity and diametrically opposed treatment of the same conduct—such as the example of the letter—is startling. Law is a local profession. International practitioners are the outliers.

Another matter involved a German company wishing to change distributors in Saudi Arabia. Here local knowledge was key. There was nothing in the parties' contract to prevent such a change, but Saudi courts usually award damages to the terminated distributor for "goodwill." If the parties were forced into court, the old distributor could claim that the foreign manufacturer's employees had been in the Kingdom under his company's immigration sponsorship, had been exposed to his trade secrets and so could be deported and barred from re-entering the Kingdom for up to two years.

"Amicable" arbitration was a possibility to help the parties get past their dispute and Saudi Arabia had even acceded to the 1958 New York Convention on the Recognition and Enforcement of Foreign Arbitration Awards. Unfortunately, despite the law, few foreign arbitral awards had ever been enforced in Saudi Arabia.

August—Green Zone

August 1

TWO RAIDS THIS EVENING. The raids always come at night. During the day the insurgents run too great a risk of being seen from the air. I went to the "Sugar Shack," to buy shaving cream, but they didn't have any. Tomorrow I will try the Iraqi market, a collection of small shops at Forward Operating Base Prosperity. Perhaps I can get a map of what is now being called the "International Zone." I think this name was cooked up by the U.S. State Department. They think removing all the terminology of conflict people will make people forget about the sirens. No one uses the new term. Everyone continues to call it the Green Zone.

★★★

The Coalition Provisional Authority, the government of the occupation, started issuing laws as soon as it was constituted. Since the Authority lacked any kind of comprehensive knowledge of Iraqi laws—and there was no post-invasion plan—

ruling by decree in coordination with United States military forces was the only alternative.

There were many businessmen who believed that there would be money to be made in a post-Saddam Iraq and they lobbied the Authority ferociously for changes in Iraqi laws that would facilitate their businesses. There was no comprehensive legal plan. To complicate matters, when the Authority was disestablished and a new Iraqi government installed, some Coalition laws were carried forward, on a law by law basis. So you would have to check and see if the new Iraqi government had permitted the Authority's laws to continue in force. Baathist institutions created under Saddam no longer existed; but older laws still in force referred to the authority of the Revolutionary Guard and the Baathist party, and it wasn't always clear whether these provisions could simply be disregarded without doing violence to the meaning of the law as a whole, or if references to the Revolutionary Guard would be interpreted as the current government or not. You could use common sense, but one lawyer's common-sense is rarely another's, especially in a war zone where two or three legal traditions were coming together.

★
★ ★

Office work continues to be a parade of one problem after another. I have a list of "To-do's" that must be done immediately. I can't finish all of them.

I am not an expert on Iraqi law. If I ask Ahmed for assistance, I might get a paragraph in two day's time. Local lawyers believe that writing a lone paragraph is an extraordinary achievement. Send that paragraph to a company like Siemens and the response is outrage. How dare you try to answer this complex question with just a paragraph? Somehow I have to bridge that gap.

Today there was another rush. I am working on a real estate contract for the government of the Netherlands. They are selling their embassy in the Red Zone because it was hit by missiles. The buyer is a political big shot who wants to take possession before the closing so that he can commence renovations. The price is approximately 1.1 million USD. There is nothing in the contract about how payment is to be made and checks aren't used here. The closing is a month away.

Even a novice lawyer knows that letting a buyer take possession of real property prior to the transfer of title is a bad idea. So many things can go wrong at the last minute. In a war zone, you are asking for trouble. But word has come down that I need to accommodate the buyer. He wants to move in immediately. Permission from the Dutch Ministry of Foreign Affairs has not yet been received and for all I know may never be received. If someone is injured on the property when renovations begin or if a wall collapses because someone backs a bulldozer into it, who will bear the risk of loss?

So I put together a bare-bones agreement with what I thought was a pretty good alternative. For $1, the buyer would be granted a thirty-day license to enter the premises with a hold harmless clause. The license would expire automatically at the end of the thirty day period unless extended in writing. So after thirty days, the buyer would becomes a trespasser if the sale for some reason did not close. The license ended up being no more than three pages long. Florian was appalled—he expected a document of at least twenty pages in length, if not more. The problem is that you can't charge that much for a three page contract, even if that is all the client needs.

One thing I did learn from Florian, is that you can charge more if your work product—whether a contract or a memorandum—has a table of contents. You can charge even more if it has both a table of contents and an index.

I also learned not to talk to the client without having him sign a document Florian titled, "Terms of Business." This was a single page form agreement for legal services. In all of our initial discussions with clients, we were to answer no questions except to say that we would be happy to answer questions after they became a client by agreeing to our Terms of Business. There are good reasons for this.

It costs money to maintain offices and clients often only call when Google and Wikipedia are silent. I was with Florian once when someone called his mobile. "Who are you?" Florian asked him, "are you a client?" After determining that the individual had not signed the Terms of Business, Florian told him in no uncertain terms that unless and until he established a relationship with us by signing there was nothing to talk about. The Terms of Business agreement is a good solution to one of the problems of an international law practice and thus frees the individual attorney from fielding unsolicited calls seeking answers to general legal questions.

There are all sorts of problems back home. Rather than simply looking after the loose ends relating to the 46th Street house sale in Miami, Donna decided that the house is not ready to be "shown." So she moved in. I made the mistake of telling her that this could be a one way trip and that I might not come back. Selling an unoccupied house is much easier than coordinating visits among a resident, a potential buyer and the realtor. This was not a good development. There are so many questions and so much needs to be done. Even with an agent, the sale of real estate is time-consuming. I am not stressed out by the war. That is the strangest thing. What continues to cause stress is the situation at home. But home is too far away.

Egyptian Distributorships

THERE WERE SO MANY matters that had nothing to do with Iraq that even from a business point of view I sometimes wondered what was the point of having me in the Green Zone. I could have commuted when needed from Abu Dhabi and worked out of the Dubai office. Another matter that had nothing to do with Iraq involved a Big Automobile Manufacturer (BAM) and its desire to circumvent its local distributor in Egypt.

BAM currently has two legal entities in Egypt, namely BAM Egypt S.A.E. ("BAME") and Little Side Business, S.A.E. ("LSB"). LSB currently imports bolt-on aftermarket kits into Egypt while BAM wants a legal assessment of the currently applicable legal framework in Egypt. Who better to answer that question than an attorney based in Baghdad? This time the Cairo office assisted by getting the appropriate Egyptian legislation to me and so answering the question was fairly straightforward.

Work was always interesting: it seemed there was always a new legal system to acquaint myself with, whether it was the United Arab Emirates, Egypt, Syria, Saudi Arabia or even—what a thought—Iraq.

It was never entirely clear to me why answering this question was beyond the ken of the Cairo office. Perhaps BAM was afraid of its local distributor getting wind of its discontent. After all, it would be extremely unlikely that the local distributor would have spies in the Green Zone. Though public espionage has captured the attention of the public, corporate espionage is much more prevalent. Given that information acquired through private espionage can be used by the Government against offenders, the Government is unlikely to crack down on offenders anytime soon. I figured that every time I tried to call Europe that more than one intelligence agency was listening in. The United States, of course, was the primary culprit. But since the United States does not share its intelligence with the Germans or the French, each of these had their own way of listening in. Not to mention Hezbollah, Syria, the Iranians and the Lebanese. Sometimes I would pick up the phone and hear a click. Like at the beginning a conference call, I was tempted to ask, "is everyone ready?" before getting started.

Given that the firm has six or seven offices I am finding it difficult to understand why I am being bombarded with one rush job after another. I am the only native English speaker in the entire six or seven office operation, so everyone wants to run their documents by me before they go out. I don't mind these reviews, but I end up rewriting a lot and without a printer it's just too easy to make proofreading mistakes while editing on a netbook.

I never really understood why I would be assigned so many matters that had nothing to do with Iraq or the work of the Iraq office. Reviewing the English of a document was one thing, but answering local law questions that arose in jurisdictions where we had large, real offices was an inefficient use of resources. The attorneys in those offices were not under fire and had resources vastly superior to mine. Was this a test? Was I being set up to fail?

The next question came out of Dubai. Though we had an office on Sheikh Zayed Road near the Sheraton Four Corners hotel, the corporate structure of MENA was byzantine. We also were established in the Dubai Free Zone where we had an office. Could a branch office of a Free Zone company sign a lease and so be established in Dubai proper?

When a question like this arose, my first thought would not be to send it to an attorney in the Green Zone who did not have access to Emirati legal materials or ministries.

When countries make local set-up difficult and free zone set-up easy, it should be no surprise that businesses will try to use the free zone to avoid the more stringent requirements of the base economy. Why no one had thought to answer this question before we rented space on Sheikh Zayed Road was the real question that needed an answer.

It surprised me that so much of the work I did in Iraq could have been comfortably accomplished while sitting in Miami. But no matter—I was happy to have the work though I thought it was odd that I would receive these assignments.

Another case involved a housing construction dispute between the government of Egypt and a developer. The government entered into a contract for a development project of two plots of land and promised substantial new public housing.

After the contract was signed, the government got cold feet. The government was under an obligation to approve or reject the developer's plans within three months of receipt. Instead, they did nothing, effectively blocking the contracted-for project. The developer, keenly feeling the loss of future rents, sued for damages. One of the developer's shareholders held Swiss nationality. There is a bilateral investment treaty between Switzerland and Egypt which could be used for dispute resolution. Fortunately, copies of the relevant treaties were available on the Internet; the procedural rules of the Egyptian administrative tribunals were not. Nevertheless, there was recent case law that counseled initiating an international arbitration, which is what we advised the client to do.

August 2

I haven't spent any money here. All my expenses are picked up by the firm; it's amazing. All I have to do is produce. On the other hand, this is a war zone.

The Arab rhythm of life isn't felt in the compound at all. There is nothing really like a 9-5 workday and every day is the same.

The fear is that the Iraqis will not be able to form a government before Ramadan and the exuberance of the holy month will cause all sorts of sectarian violence.

I was able to convince Donna to let the realtor handle the sale. She gave the keys to Max so she is out of the house. I don't know what's left there. Whatever remains will have to be abandoned.

According to the Iraqi government, July was the deadliest month for attacks in two years. The United States has announced that its troops will withdraw on schedule. All troops will be gone by the end of 2011. But that's not entirely true: all combat troops will be gone, but 50,000 regulars will remain for training missions. These are the same soldiers, the only difference is in their mission. Al-Qaeda will not make a distinction between combat troops and military advisors. The Viet Cong did not either. In fact, the entire Viet Nam war was fought by those same military advisors. I don't have a good feeling about this at all.

August 3

Sirens at 3 a.m. I didn't hear any explosions.

Today I saw the Tigris river, which curves around the the Green Zone. The river seems to be shallow. Dredges were working and there was no river traffic. To the east is downtown Baghdad. Crossing the river means entering the Red Zone. The Red Zone is the unknown, the wilderness: bat country.

Bernhard Dolinek agreed to show me around. He is the resident Daimler representative. He has a good deal of experience in the Middle East and was familiar with Daimler's sales set-up in Saudi Arabia. More importantly, he had been in the Green Zone for a while and was very knowledgeable.

We left the Sabre compound around mid-morning. The car's doors were heavy, it is an armored B-6 vehicle, driven by Duncan Burns, the Scottish soldier whom I met last night. The roads are in terrible condition. It is here that the war took place, where the Americans destroyed when they conquered, but because the fighting never stopped never paused to rebuild.

We passed the Four Soldiers monument near the compound in the middle of a roundabout placed in the center of what was once a wide boulevard. The formal name of the statute is the July 14th Monument and it honors soldiers who perished in the revolution to overthrow the monarchy on July 14, 1958. Not everyone is familiar with Iraqi history and more than one person told me that the monument was a tribute to those fallen in the Iraq-Iran war, but this is not the case.

Seven years after the war started, the boulevard is still littered with war debris. Traffic lights do not function. There are no lane markers and cars dodge each other as they make their way through traffic. We focus so much on the current war that we forget that there have been two other recent wars. The war with Iran lasted eight years and this one is not yet finished.

Bombed-out buildings have not been repaired. Instead they have been surrounded by blast walls and abandoned. They are the reminders of a war that has not ended.

In this section of the Green Zone there is a little, but very little, commercial activity. Near the monument there is a Chinese restaurant that has been built inside a 40 foot shipping container. A 20 foot shipping container has been repurposed and is now a pharmacy. The owner is the son of a former Iraqi army general. He is the only one permitted to sell medicines in the Green Zone. Few things have changed, really, in the new Iraq.

The same general also owns the only gas station. It is inside a former villa. Gasoline and diesel are dispensed through hoses hanging from raised 55 gallon drums. Because of the unreliability of electricity, gravity must do all the work.

We pass the U.S. Embassy compound. There

is a sports field inside. This month, two men were killed there in a rocket attack. The Embassy is the target drawing rockets from the Red Zone.

The Fedex licensee is a company called GSI Business Services. Like many other businesses in the Green Zone, they are housed in what used to be a residence. The Fedex office is on the other side of the boulevard from the pharmacy and part of it look like it too started life as a shipping container.

As I had feared, the office address given me in Baghdad was only partially correct. How can someone not know their own address? Partly because they never go to the office.

Social life here is non-existent. This is no different than prison. Iraq is quite a jump from Florida. I shouldn't pretend to have a foot in both places because I do not.

August 5 1 a.m.

Can't sleep. Max wants to talk. I was hoping to keep family issues, personal issues and such out of this diary but perhaps they are going to slip in anyway.

I can't help Max. Away at college, he is very much alone. We're talking on the phone everyday and that helps somewhat, but there have been technical problems on both ends so the communications are difficult. Nevertheless, we are able to stay in touch despite the difficulties. While we are on the phone or chatting on the computer, we are both visiting a place called the Internet. While there, our physical location doesn't matter. When we hang up, he returns to his life in the United States, while I find myself in a war zone. This is sometimes bewildering.

Another night with no rocket attack alarms. The wireless wasn't working this morning, but the ethernet connection was. I was able to download a book about Islamic finance by Dr. Yahya Al-Samaan, a Saudi academic whom I had known in Riyadh. Tomorrow is Friday though this means nothing: work continues as usual.

Last Friday I was still jet-lagged. I guess I'll use the time to catch-up, but I'd rather not sit around doing nothing. I don't know how safe it is to walk over to the Fedex office. I still don't have my badges, telephone, business cards or freedom of movement. The fact is the firm was not ready for me.

A software setting was preventing me from accessing the Microsoft Exchange Server in Dubai. I had to research the issue, edit the computer's registry, and then and only then was I able to connect. MENA should have given me the settings in Dubai rather than just entering them in my laptop.

I went up to the gym and exercised for twenty-five minutes yesterday. One half-hour is within reach. The gym is never empty; there are always people working out, both the younger guys as well as the older ones. I see Duncan again, as well as a few other familiar faces.

An inquiry came up concerning service of process in Iraq for an Australian court case. Service of process in wartime is an interesting subject. Because of the uncertainty as to what laws apply there can be unintended legal consequences. The key case on foreign extraditions in the United States is *Kerr v. Illinois* which arose out of an effort by bounty hunters to bring back a fugitive from Peru. Peru was under Chilean military occupation during the War of the Pacific and there were no Peruvian authorities to authorize extradition to the United States. Service of Australian process in Iraq is governed by a 1933 treaty between the United Kingdom and Iraq. It is unclear whether private process servers could be used. I told the client that he could go ahead and try. I wouldn't want to try to serve process in a country overrun with militias.

I thought I would have enough free time so as to be able to finish the Tuduj appellate brief. The brief will be due thirty days after the Record is filed—though when that will be, no one knows. It could be tomorrow, it could be a year from now. American criminal cases are like that. Given my current circumstances, I do not see how I will be able to finish the brief—or even get a copy of the Record on Appeal. This is just not the place to complete such a task, not with the deadline after deadline environment I am in and an intermittent Internet connection.

The Case of the Missing Chicken

HOW DO YOU HIDE 10,000 tons of chicken?

Kitchens are just as important to armies as bullets. With Iraq in ruins, the Coalition Provisional Authority purchased 25,000 tons of chicken from a Jordanian company called Provimi. But Provimi delivered only 15,000 tons called for by the contract.

The first few shipments were without incident. The chicken left Amman, the capital of Jordan, in ten truck convoys headed to the Iraqi border. Between Amman and the border there is just one road to follow; the drivers were Iraqis who had their own trucks or rented them on the open market. The Jordanian customs authorities found no irregularities with the export of the chicken from Jordan. From the border to Baghdad, there are several possible routes. After crossing the border, there was no way to trace the chicken.

In September, 2004, another convoy of chicken convoy left Amman for Baghdad. The drivers were to carry the chicken to a warehouse operated by the Iraqi Ministry of Agriculture. When they arrived at the warehouse in Baghdad, they were told that the warehouse was full and they should take the chicken to a new location where it could be offloaded.

The drivers offloaded the chicken and were given receipts. This happened one hundred fourteen times before the Iraqi Ministry of Agriculture realized that someone had been stealing their chicken. Worse, the drivers could not remember the locations of the unfamiliar new offload sites. 8800 tons of chicken worth five million dollars was gone.

The Ministry of Agriculture told the U.S. Army—the successor to the CPA—that the chicken had not been received at government warehouses and so the amounts owed Provimi for the undelivered chicken should not be paid.

When Provimi was notified of the U.S. government action they protested because the chicken had in fact been delivered. They wisely had kept the receipts given the drivers at the sham warehouses. Meanwhile, 8800 tons of illegal chicken entered Iraqi markets. The thieves were smart, and the chicken hijacking accomplished on an industrial scale. The level of planning was extensive. The thieves had to fake warehouse receipts, they had to have the Ministry of Agriculture's own warehouse guard direct the trucks to the new locations and they needed the people at the real destination to keep their mouths shut. The problem in stealing 8800 tons of chicken isn't merely offloading, it is also what to do with it afterwards. This was not a matter of slipping a few plucked birds into street markets for the occasional dinar. Selling the stolen chicken was a massive commercial operation.

When the U.S. government advised Provimi that the remaining invoices for the 114 truckloads

The Case of the Missing Chicken

of chicken would not be paid, Provimi filed a claim against the U.S. government. U.S. government contract law is different from customary contract law because of the unequal position of the parties. The government has rights that private parties do not. The government has set up special administrative law rules to manage disputes that arise under its contracts and a system of administrative tribunals to hear appeals from the system. But appeal to the Armed Services Board of Contract Appeals was not required in this case. The government negotiated a settlement with Provimi. That took a year. On December 31, 2005, the case settled. Five years went by.

In September, 2010, the Iraqi State Company for Agriculture Sales sued Provimi in a local Iraqi court. The Iraqi government-controlled company was not a signatory to either the original contract or the compromise and settlement five years earlier. No matter. They sued anyway.

It would be easy to say that their lawsuit involved the efforts of an Iraqi government agency to seek damages arising from a performed contract to which it was not a party. The Coalition Provisional Authority no longer exists. The U.S. government has compromised and settled the claim in full. Provimi should have been in the clear.

But nothing is clear in Iraq. Provimi had done business in Iraq and so it was subject to Iraqi jurisdiction. Iraq's courts are courts of general jurisdiction. The value of the chicken was enough to meet the court's jurisdictional requirement as well, a mere 500 dinars.

Moreover, Iraqi law states that Iraqi law shall apply to contracts concluded in Iraq, and this one was. The statute of limitations for this kind of case under Iraqi law is stated in Article 244 of the Civil Code: three years. It had been six years since the chicken had been stolen, but only a year and a half since the U.S. ceased to be the occupier.

An Iraqi court could well hold that the statute of limitations was suspended during wartime, and that would make the claim timely. Assuming that Provimi was a U.S. government contractor in 2004—a fair analysis—it no longer enjoyed immunity from suit since that immunity was abolished by the U.S.-Iraq Status of Forces Agreement, effective January 1, 2009. Ironically, it would be up to an Iraqi court to enforce that grant of immunity.

Iraq recognizes the concept of *res judicata*. According to Article 81 of the Civil Action law, repeated litigation is prohibited. Claimants only get one bite at the apple.But since the plaintiff had not been a party to either the contract or its settlement, this was not a bar to the lawsuit either.

We expected that the case would move forward. We advised the client to raise all possible defenses and try to dismiss the case based on immunity. We recommended that the U.S. or the Iraqi Ministry of Justice be approached in order to file a suggestion of immunity. We could file an action seeking cover from Provimi's insurers. We could file a counterclaim—after all, Provimi was not at fault. The Ministry of Agriculture should have exercised better control. We expected that all these preliminary matters would take up to a year to resolve. Presumably Ahmed would be available to appear in court, or one of my yet unidentified and unmet colleagues in the Red Zone.

This case fairly represents the spectrum of legal issues an international law practice faces in Iraq. There are different rules under different legal systems. U.S. administrative law was once used and may now be applicable. The usages of war apply to the circumstances at the time of the threat. There are agencies that no longer exist, a grant of immunity that must be enforced by a court system that was against the grant in the first place. After a clash between different sovereigns, one greatly more powerful than the other, while neither had complete control. An innocent foreign company is left holding the bag. And all over missing chicken.

Only certain companies and individuals bought chicken on this scale. These were the same people who regularly bought this quantity of chicken legally. The same people who purchased illegal chicken were the people who purchased legal chicken. It could happen no other way. These people were still in business and still doing business with the Ministry. The Ministry knew who they were. It is their business to know. The theft had been successful. Maybe there were people in the Ministry who didn't get their cut, or were jealous that the buyers had profited. The Iraqi government lawsuit was just another attempt at theft in a country in which everyone had their hand out.

August 6

THERE WAS AN attack last night and another one this evening. The more I look the more this place seems to be a total disaster. Tariq Aziz, Saddam's foreign minister, is begging the Americans to stay. He says that if they leave they will be "abandoning Iraq to the wolves." One of the young Iraqis who works at the Graphics Department next door tells me that if anyone sees me in the Red Zone they will shoot me. I thanked him for the warning.

So I will never be a part of this place. How long will my tenure last? Three years?

Today I worked on a transaction involving an Egyptian company and the municipality of Budva in Montenegro. The plans involve building a five-star luxury hotel with additional commercial properties and a marina. There are plans for a condo hotel, a business model that has seen hard times in the United States.

A developer wanted to sign a joint venture to develop a high-end five star hotel with accompanying mixed use residential real estate in Budva, Montenegro. We represented one of the developers, backed by private Yemeni financing. The transaction has nothing to do with Iraq. The agreement's governing law was Switzerland. Legal review of the joint venture agreement was needed immediately.

The project was to be a resort and would boast, in addition to the hotel, beach facilities, a spa and wellness center, medical facilities, shops, restaurants, sports and a marina. The Yemeni backers would put up roughly one-quarter of the cost of the development in cash. The backers were a privately owned family business and like many such enterprises in the Middle East, had no financial statements. Still, financial statements are needed when credit is needed. When credit is not an issue, neither are financial statements. The problem is that the lenders want documents that do not exist.

I could be working on this matter from anywhere. So why do they have me here? The legal profession is still uncomfortable with attorneys working remotely. In the future it will be common.

The planned resort certainly was impressive. It looked like a nice place to take a vacation. It certainly would be a nicer place than the Green Zone.

August 7

There was only one alarm last night, but it was followed by some kind of broadcast on the alarm system. I couldn't make out the words, which seemed to be in English. There was no follow-up, so the broadcast couldn't have been that important.

Iraq is still torn by war. There are daily "de-Baathification" trials in the Green Zone, where defendants are tried for crimes against humanity.

Tariq Aziz was Saddam's foreign minister and he is attending these trials, though it is not clear if he is a defendant or participating in some other fashion. The new Iraqi legal system has inherited from the Americans the tendency to drag legal proceedings out endlessly. Who is defending these men? Who are their lawyers? These cases are precisely the kind that call out for the participation of qualified international criminal defense lawyers. Yet there are none present.

Several Western doctors were killed yesterday in Afghanistan. In Baghdad, several traffic policemen were murdered. Traffic policemen carry no weapons here, if attacked, they cannot fight back. They have a crucial role to play because there are no working traffic lights. Electricity is sporadic. The wires have been taken. Without the traffic policemen traffic would be even more chaotic.

There is cable television in my room, with both

Iraqi and a few international channels. I watched the Kurdish channel for a while, the Kurdish language was displayed in the Roman alphabet; the language sounds nothing like Arabic. Iranian television carried a translated press conference from Beirut. Hassan Nasrallah, the head of Hezbollah, was presenting evidence to show that Israel was responsible for killing Rafik Hariri, the former prime minister of Lebanon. He used evidence that would have been admitted in federal court under F.R.E. 404(b) (evidence of past acts to show conformity therewith) and made a convincing case. I have seen people convicted on less evidence in federal court. The International Tribunal disagrees with him; hopefully they have stronger evidence. It seemed strange to watch a Hezbollah program on Iranian television while inside the heart of American military power.

August 8

The violence continues. Forty-three dead after a blast in Basra. Car bomb? Does it make a difference? Florian says that we are going to open an office there nevertheless. Perhaps that office can be dedicated to Montenegrin cases. The security situation sucks. The first explosion was a car bomb; the second came from a bomb placed next to a power generator. In Ramadi, seventy miles to the south of Baghdad, people were waiting in line outside the post office when a suicide bomber detonated his explosive vest. Eight were killed and twenty-three were wounded.

Florian is dreaming if he thinks the security situation will be better in three months.

August 9

Since the phone wasn't working, I thought I would walk over to Fedex to see if my new typewriter had arrived. I reached the main road leading to the Four Soldiers monument. Russian security forces were hanging around two black Chevrolet Suburbans. On a wall there was a poster advertising shipping container remodeling. The business was located inside the sole Iraqi police station in the Green Zone. There was a lot of traffic on the road, black SUV's with flashing lights that stopped for no one. One of them had a general officer plaque on top of the dashboard, a red square with two gold stars. But it was likely the car wasn't assigned to a general at all. Ahmed told me that these vehicles were used by the FBI or the CIA. If Ahmed knows this, so do all the Iraqis, including our friends in Al-Qaeda.

As I continued along the black asphalt street on the way to Fedex, I saw a giant crane loading another mortar shelter inside the walled-in yard of the Iraqi government mine-removal office. This is not a good sign at all. The agency is behind a ten foot high blast wall topped with barbed wire. They are still preparing for mortar attacks even now.

The typewriter hadn't arrived, but there was a package of mail for me. I left to walk back and stopped at the Freedom Restaurant and Supermarket, next to the only pharmacy. Forty glum Iraqis sitting inside stopped what they were doing and looked up at me. These were looks of surprise; not too many Americans ever stop there. Americans don't normally patronize the Freedom Restaurant. The diners were joyless, despite their new freedoms.

There were shelves lining the interior walls of the Freedom Restaurant. I couldn't place the construction—it could have been a series of shipping containers, or it could have been some kind of purpose-built facility. None of the products were Iraqi, but China and Turkey were well-represented. I didn't buy anything and continued the walk back to the compound. I passed an electrical junction box—it had been completely stripped of wiring. What was left was a steel box with nothing inside. Who would take the wires? When there are few ways to make a living scrounging for scrap metal is an option. Fixing the traffic lights will require much more than replacing burnt-out bulbs and flipping a power switch.

Last night there was one alarm. I do not know if mortars were fired.

I saw Dr. von Traven of the German Trade office at dinner in the Sabre mess hall. He has just returned from Basra. He told me that the press had played down the recent attacks. He said there were three car bombs and not two and over one hundred people were killed. The bombs were detonated on a busy, pedestrian-filled street. When I told Ahmed al-Jabali that the Americans were leaving on August 30, he told me that this might explain why the streets are so empty.

We have broken Baghdad and left her to her fate. The people are afraid. Those that are committing acts of violence are coordinating their efforts. The army is weak. Iraq used to be a highly civilized country, a normal country. It isn't any more.

Three mortar explosions so far this evening.

August 10

There was only one bomb blast this evening. It came around 8 p.m. while I was in the cafeteria. The insurgency goes on and the government is in no position to stop it. Months after the election, there still is no functioning government. The country cannot even agree on the start of Ramadan. The Sunni say it starts tomorrow but the shi'a, following Grand Ayatollah Sistani, say it starts the day after tomorrow and those who follow Moqtada al-Sadr have chosen the day after that.

I am waiting on mail that hasn't yet arrived. I

cannot complain, this is the life that I have chosen to lead. Once I was a soldier in the drug war, a war that was never fought. And now I am here in the middle of a real war.

All the criticism I have put up with over the years due to my working in Saudi Arabia will disappear now that I am in Iraq. No one will dare question anything, no one will dare criticize. It is a small price to pay for normalcy, for acceptance: an unexpected silencing of critics.

But if the insurgents improve their targeting none of this will matter.

The Project Negotiating Mandate

WHEN APPROACHED BY a client with a new matter, sometimes it is difficult to determine the real nature of the problem. The advice sought may be fairly straightforward, but the facts are often hidden. Human nature being what it is, eventually things become clear. Agency issues recur and require legal intervention. When a law forbids or restricts a practice for commercial or protectionist reasons, a tremendous amount of effort goes into seeking ways around the law.

For foreign lawyers, commercial agency issues are initially mysterious. I once asked an American firm if they would like to contribute an article to a newsletter on the subject. I thought it would be refreshing to have a contribution from the point of view of attorneys who represented the foreign company that needed to appoint a local representative. Instead I received an informative irrelevant, article on the topic of principal and agent. They just didn't get it.

In much of the Middle East, companies are forbidden from entering the retail market directly. The only way to sell their products is by appointing a local national or company as sales agent. Because of globalization pressures, these countries have had to abandon their wholly protectionist policies for deceptive ones. That is, they have amended their laws so that they can say that foreigners are not prohibited from trading, but at the same time they have enacted onerous entry requirements for foreign companies. Foreign companies will then do everything in their power to avoid appointing an agent. If they could square the circle or turn apples into oranges, they would do so.

One day Florian sent a fifty page document to me for review. It was drafted under UAE law, which has a similar agency regime as the rest of the Gulf Cooperation Council Countries. I am not sure why the team in Dubai was unable to work on the matter. I asked myself what this task had to do with Iraq or the Baghdad office because I couldn't see any connection.

The document was titled, "Project Negotiating

The Project Negotiating Mandate 85

Mandate." I had never seen such a document and was not sure what was being negotiated, since the project negotiator, according to the terms of the contract, would in fact have no power to negotiate anything. I read through the document once and still had no idea what it was about. Complicating matters, the author of the document was not a native English speaker. I have no idea what language gave birth to the text, but it wasn't until the third reading that I realized the true nature of the document. As I had suspected, there were no projects to negotiate, but there were sales to be made. The project negotiator would not be paid a salary, but would derive a commission from each sale made, after the parent company had received funds from the buyer, who was given some equally obscure title. The agency law of the Emirates was specifically stated not to apply, since only projects were being negotiated. Needless to say, the document skirted all of the local law protections for national agents. Since the agreement was only a project negotiating mandate, how could those horrible protectionist sales agent laws apply?

The client was crestfallen when he learned that his creative use of Google Translate and a thesaurus had failed to yield a way around national legislation. I hated to give him the bad news. My guess is that Florian had told him that "project negotiating mandates" would pass muster under UAE law. Of course, if there had been projects to negotiate in the first place, Florian would probably be right.

I could have answered this question while seated comfortably in Dubai, or for that matter, Miami. I don't believe the firm would be in a position to charge extra due to the fact that the responsible attorney was in Iraq in a war zone. I am sure that there is an answer to this question. Someday I may learn why.

August 11

One alarm this morning. It came about 4:00 a.m. I didn't hear any explosions. At breakfast no one mentions it. There is no news.

It was 53 degrees centigrade yesterday, (127° F). Is that even possible? It is unspeakably hot. The air conditioners at the compound are running at full blast but in some rooms are having difficulty keeping up.

In the meantime, we forge ahead with our plans. Will more business come our way? This has yet to be seen.

I am using my personal diary in the office because I don't have anything else to use. Without access badges I am stuck here at Sabre. With all the heat it is hard to go anywhere by foot. Perhaps I will be able to get away for Eid. Five days in Europe would be great.

August 12

General Babaker Zebari, the head of the Iraqi Army, says that the army will not be ready to take over from the Americans until 2020. But the Americans are going anyway. This means, quite simply, that all hell will break loose.

Florian told me that one of the people I would be working with was Amir Kordvani, an Iranian attorney who spoke Arabic, English and German. I thought it was great that I would be getting some help, until he mentioned that he wasn't in Baghdad, but was working out of his home in Australia due to "passport problems." In fact there was no passport problem, Amir simply had to complete a term of residency in Australia to qualify for citizenship there. How long would it take? At least another year. So there would be no Australian boots on the ground in the short term.

There was another problem. Amir was Iranian, and Iran had finished a war against Iraq not too long ago. It wasn't that long ago that the Ayatollah Khomeini sent Iranian suicide troops to march on Iraqi positions. The Iraqis hate the Iranians because they were at war with their country for eight years. But the enemy of my enemy is my friend. I am seen as an enemy as well, especially now that I have an LoA.

I wondered how Amir and Ahmed would get

along. The shi'a/sunni rift was widening daily. In the Middle East, memories run deep. Ahmed had already told me that he did not regret Saddam's invasion of Kuwait. Kuwait was nothing more than a renegade Iraqi province. One day they would take it back. What he regretted was that the Americans had arrived and taken Kuwait out of Saddam's hands, especially after having given him the tacit go-ahead by having the U.S. ambassador at the time tell him that Iraqi-Kuwaiti relations were an internal Iraqi domestic matter. That was all Saddam needed to hear.

August 13

There was a test of the bomb warning system today. I walked to the Fedex office. Two defense contractors were hanging out in the office. Lianna, the office manager, had gone to the airport and wasn't there. They had my Fedex package. This one was sent from Dubai: office goodies, stationery.

I took a picture of the bomb shelter on the football field and posted it on Facebook. My friends must think I'm crazy. No one commented.

Just like in prison, I've been starting to look forward to meal times. I'd love to have a glass of champagne. I haven't had anything to drink since I got here.

I've got to stay sharp.

The U.S. Ambassador left today. He was unsuccessful in getting the Iraqis to form a new government. The task will be left for his replacement. It will be a while before the new guy can get up to speed. That's the problem with Department of State personnel—by the time they can absorb enough local knowledge to be effective, they are transferred to another post so they do not become "advocates" for the foreign country. Then the cycle begins again with a new incumbent.

Ramadan here isn't so bad. Iraq was once a secular country. The Muslims eat during the day and think nothing of it. There was once even a thriving Jewish community in Iraq, but not anymore.

August 15

I worked out for thirty minutes today after a break yesterday. The amazing thing is that I'm probably living healthier here than in Miami.

A friend of mine slipped in an e-mail and told my mother that I am in Baghdad. So to keep her from worrying, I had to lie. Not much of a choice there. This is what lawyers do, after all.

There was one siren this evening, about ten p.m. I didn't hear any explosions. I wonder if the insurgents believe they scared off the U.S. Ambassador. I've already become blasé about the attacks.

The house is still an issue—there were simply too many things that I could not finish before I left. Sitting here in Baghdad, none of this really matters. I paid for storage six months in advance. I suppose I'll go home for the holidays, but where is home?

I arrived here in wartime. Whatever it is I felt I had to prove, I have proven it. I am here at the time of the rockets. My old life is over.

August 15

A memo went out with the wrong client's name buried on page 29 of a document. Awful. Embarrassing. But how am I supposed to review documents on a netbook? We don't have a printer to print them. The screen is too small. Nevertheless, it is my responsibility. I don't need mistakes like this.

The insurgents are waiting. Saddam's army. Saddam's intelligence services. They are all waiting. They are waiting for the Americans to leave. After they leave, they will settle scores. And there will be no one to stop them.

August 16

The military reports that an unmanned drone crashed in Central Iraq. Yesterday, two people were killed and five wounded when a minibus hit a roadside bomb in Baghdad—they are using roadside bombs still in Baghdad—and a police officer was killed when a bomb placed under his vehicle detonated. On Saturday, two policemen were shot and killed while they slept in their patrol car. Then the car was lit on fire.

The two candidates for prime minister, Nouri al-Maliki and Ayad Allawi, cannot form a government. One political party won 91 seats, the other 89. Both want to be prime minister. The United States still has this country under military occupation but the storyline is that the war is over. Their attention is drifting elsewhere. Afghanistan has the attention of the public. Iraq is old news.

Meanwhile, in Iraq the insurgency steps into the vacuum. The violence will escalate. The insurgents wait for a draw-down of American power. There are scores to settle.

★★★

I took a few pictures around the compound and posted them on Facebook. There is a lot of work but things are improving. I should get my military identification cards soon.

I learned that the old saw about the French Foreign Legion as a tool to help you forget is not true. The opposite is true. With this sensory deprivation all you have are your memories. These memories become more intense. I look at the people who have stayed in touch with me—it's really a small number.

My health is pretty good. I think that I have a hernia from moving boxes in Miami. I have been losing weight. This experience has been good for me, despite the reality of the situation—after all I am in a war zone. The combat helmet is in the closet if I need it. The sirens warning of rocket attacks sound at night. And I am alone.

You think of odd things while under fire. I wonder if this diary has magical properties: that I will live until all of its pages are filled in. I wonder.

Today there were no e-mails about the house. There were no e-mails of any kind. It is a relief, no recriminations, peace.

August 17

What a day. Around the time I was having my morning coffee, a suicide bomber entered a police recruiting station, one of the safest places in Baghdad. He blew himself up; 61 people were killed. In the morning, I heard machine gun fire. Repeatedly. Maybe it was only practice, but I had not heard that sound here before. Around 9 p.m. there was an explosion and the sirens went off. Mortar fire. It was close. I was still in the office.

The situation here is utterly unstable. It will only get worse. Now there's talk of Israel attacking Iran in order to destroy one of the nuclear reactors that Iran has under construction. If there is an Israeli attack there will be repercussions here.

Max is returning to Chicago this week and has done more of the things I asked him to do.

Last night there were noises coming from the dropped ceiling and I thought there might be insects. But the noises were too loud for just crawling insects. I couldn't sleep and at one point while sleeping on my stomach I felt something walk across my back. At first I thought it might be a gecko or some other lizard. But I'm not in Miami, are there even geckos in the desert?

Then I felt the fur.

When I came downstairs from the office this evening I could hear something scratching inside the dresser. I opened all the drawers, but there was nothing. A few minutes later a rat ran out and escaped by crawling under the door. About an hour later, the rat came back, but left when I made a noise. Now I have shoes blocking the door. If the rat wanted to, he could easily push them aside.

Florian complained about a memorandum I wrote. He rarely likes anything I write. It's hard enough trying to guess what the client wants. Be general. Be specific. Change upon change: after ten drafts my eyes glaze over. For the past two days he's been carrying on suggesting that I should consider joint stock companies in the opinion. I spoke to him on the phone and he urged me to expand the advice memorandum by changing our recommendation in favor of joint stock companies. I ended up spending the entire day on the memorandum and I'm still not finished.

I finally added a section on joint stock companies and took out other parts of the memorandum that were inconsistent with the new position. I did a 180-degree turn and expressed what I thought was Florian's point of view. After reading the memorandum, Florian now says that maybe joint stock companies are a bad idea after all. He hates to be seen as indecisive but in this legal environment precision is aspirational at best. If remove them from the memo no doubt he'll be back in a couple of days suggesting they be added.

They asked me today where my salary should be sent. I suppose that's a good sign, but all afternoon I had visions of getting fired. That's all I need. My imagined obituary: "Not even good enough to keep a job in a war zone." How pathetic.

August 18

Prime Minister Allawi came to the Sabre compound around lunchtime. I noticed that something was up when I came downstair from the office and ran into a soldier waiting with a machine gun at the bottom of the staircase.

At 2:38 there was an explosion from a mortar round. This time I felt it. It was close. Too close. They must have known Allawi was coming, but their timing was off.

But I kept on working.

August 19

The remaining U.S. combat troops left last night, ahead of schedule. They left in the dark to avoid attacks or reprisals. This explains the Ambassador's recent departure. The United States did the same thing when pulling out of the Canal Zone. The State Department must have a turnover manual somewhere in its files.

The war has officially lasted for seven and a half years, just short of the term of the Iraq-Iran war.

The Americans are dreaming if they think the war is over. 50,000 troops remain. If they are not combat troops, what are they? This was the Viet Nam mission. They called it the MACV, the Miltary Assistance Command-Viet Nam. Now they're saying the State Department will be in charge of training the police. It's madness, they don't know what they are doing and continue to make it up as they go along.

Between the attacks you think about the past. Seven and half years ago it was March, 2003. My life was very different. I was married. We had just had our house warming party. I had just spent one week in the U.S. I was looking for a way—any way—to come home permanently. But it was not to be. Sitting here alone past events replay themselves, one after another. What could I have done differently?

The reports of bombings don't come in all at once. There was a bombing of a kerosene truck yesterday, the same day the police recruits were murdered. So add eight more people to yesterday's death toll. Who is doing this? The Sunni Al-Qaeda? Or just a general insurgency? Maybe this insurgency is becoming a civil war.

★★★

I spent the day revising our Iraqi law guide. The assignment was overdue; it should have been finished a while ago. I finished revising the document at 7:00 p.m. or so; I didn't even have time to exercise. Because yesterday I was finishing an assignment that had to get finished that day and the day before that I was finishing an assignment that had to get finished that day. Florian's deadlines are unrealistic. Without a law library or any assistance meeting deadlines is very difficult.

I have been working so hard I haven't gotten a chance to think about myself: what am I doing here?

August 20

After rushing to meet all of yesterday's deadlines, today was a good day. I got my military credentials document, called a "Letter of Authorization" or in military-speak, "LoA." I had expected that I would get PX privileges, but it's better than that, I get APO privileges as well. Some of the additional permissions are real surprises:

Authorized weapons	Dining Facilities
Post Exchange	Military Banking
Military Mail	Airlift
Recreational Facilities	
Resuscitative Care	Transportation

Now, that is remarkable. This should make life here so much easier. I have to sign up and get a postal box ASAP as well as find out where the post office is.

Military post exchange, commissary and postal services are prized benefits made available to active duty military and contractors. When the Canal Zone was disestablished, U.S. citizen Panama Canal employees lost access to those privileges. The loss quickly became a topic, if not the only topic, of conversation among PanCanal employees who mourned not so much the sovereignty turnover as the fact that they could no longer get U.S. ham or turkey locally. In those pre-Internet days, having access to U.S. mail was vital. The loss of military privileges was a sad event. To think that all these years after Panama, I am getting privileges again: it's rather amazing. There are Morale, Welfare and Entertainment facilities; there is even a bowling alley. There are some restrictions on the use of military aircraft to and from Iraq; essentially I would be flying standby in line behind everyone else. My guess is that Florian would take a dim view of me leaving the Green Zone, never mind bouncing around Iraq in military aircraft.

There is one disturbing grant in the authorization letter: I am authorized to carry firearms. I hope I don't need them.

I had to work today, as usual. There was a meeting with a Korean delegation from a large Korean conglomerate.

Corruption in Iraq

IRAQ UNDER SADDAM was perhaps the least corrupt country in the world. There was swift, sure, and extraordinarily harsh punishment under the old regime. During Saddam's time, stories about the execution of government officials for taking money or gifts were commonplace. Commercial activities which presented significant opportunities for bribery were banned. For example, under the Commercial Agencies law, a person who acts as local agent for a foreign company and who attempts to win a State contract could be sentenced to life imprisonment. Saddam would only do business with parent companies. He did what the parent companies had always wanted to do: completely bypass the local agent. I heard one story about a judge who had refused a cup of coffee offered to him during a conference to avoid even the hint of wrongdoing.

Today there is an epidemic of corruption. Bribery is commonplace: it is every man for himself. A 2006 report by the World Bank found that Iraq's procurement procedures and practices were not in line with generally accepted public procurement practices, such as effective bid protest mechanisms and transparency on final contract awards.

Corruption is a particularly difficult legal problem because of the extraterritorial reach of some country's laws, particularly those of the United States. The United States has no problem in criminalizing conduct committed by its citizens outside its borders. The Department of Justice investigates violations of the Foreign Corrupt Practices Act (FCPA). The FCPA applies to any person—regardless of nationality—or any corporation that has its principal place of business in the United States, or which is organized under the laws of a State of the United States or a territory, possession, or commonwealth of the United States. The FCPA does not contain any threshold amount.

An American businessman would be wise not to offer an Iraqi official that cup of coffee. Nevertheless, there is a quid pro quo requirement. That is, in exchange for the bribe, the official is expected to perform some favor, bend a rule or overlook missing paperwork—or even grant a no-bid contract. For this reason, American companies are very careful. I was asked to review a case for one of those companies.

The Big American Oil Company (BAOC) set up a joint venture with the Iraqi South Oil Company, one of the country's state-owned enterprises active in the oil sector. BAOC normally paid a $1000 allowance to its board members for each meeting. The company never made clear exactly what this allowance was for. Since the Iraqi board members were government employees, BAOC asked if they could still pay them the allowance.

In 2007 two employees of the Ministry of the Interior were prosecuted for taking a bribe of only $700. Under Iraqi law, one of the definitions of corruption was any act by an employee "exceeding the limits of his job." These "limits" could be interpreted as adding to his salary without authorization. A recently passed code of conduct prohibited public employees from misusing their position to acquire personal benefits. The Iraqi Penal Code prohibits employees from accepting funds from third parties. Iraq's Civil Code even permits a person from whom a bribe is solicited to recover damages from the official soliciting the bribe.

To enforce these laws, there are several entities which investigate corruption in Iraq. The CPA created the Commission on Integrity, an agency whose continued existence is confirmed by the Iraqi constitution. In addition there is the Board of Supreme Audit, which was established in 1927. As such, it is older than the Iraqi republic itself. There are also inspectors general in each ministry working together through a Joint Anti-Corruption Council.

The United States created a special Inspector General to account for funds appropriated for the reconstruction of Iraq. Violations are also within the jurisdiction of any agency that has made grants or provided goods or services.

My conclusion after researching all of this was that the Big American Oil Company could pay all of its board members a per diem meeting allowance without violating American law.

This is the kind of matter that overseas lawyers are particularly good at analyzing because of our familiarity with different legal systems.

Forward Operating Base Union III

ARMED WITH MY LoA, I reserved a trip to FOB Union III. Ahmed came along with a friend. There are several checkpoints to pass, but with my LoA there should be no difficulty in getting through.

FOB Union was the site of the former Ba'ath party headquarters. The tomb of Michael Aflaq, the founder of the party, rests inside a blue-domed mosque-like structure on the base. Republican Guard troops were billeted there as well.

With Saddam gone, the base has been taken over by U.S. military and contractors. Private security companies like Triple Canopy provide the first line of defense. We pass through a military checkpoint where a sign advises that deadly force is authorized. This checkpoint is manned by Peruvian ex-military. It gets us near the official entrance to the U.S. Embassy. I am told that roughly 5,000 people live on the Embassy grounds. No wonder it is such an inviting target. It is about two kilometers from my compound. This is important because it means we are relatively far from the insurgent's target.

We drive to the right past the checkpoint. The twenty foot high blast walls funnel us into a single lane. The embassy is on our left. The property continues for two or three blocks. Then we reach Forward Base Union III. On our right is a filling station, another single lane with a few pumps and a gas line of motorists waiting their turn. This country was once a major oil producer but now fuel is scarce. Two gasoline trucks are parked outside the blast walls, away from the pumps.

We park the car and walk through the first checkpoint for the base. The blast walls are so narrow now that only two men can walk abreast, there's isn't enough room for a vehicle. We come to a yellow awning that provides shade from the sun.

Underneath uniformed African mercenaries lounge, accompanied by their weapons. They are from Uganda. Our arrival brings them to attention. We could be insurgents. They have their orders. They scrutinize our documents. They question my Iraqi companions in English: what is your business on the base? They answer that they are with me. I have a LoA. We are authorized.

We are all frisked for weapons and they let us pass. We walk perhaps another 200 feet and then blast walls stop us. There is a foot path to the right and an office fashioned from a discarded shipping container. We climb up two or three wooden steps. Inside two Africans await us. We show them our documents and they hold up a black device to our faces. At first I thought that they were just going to take our picture. But then I can see my eye reflected in a mirror. They are focusing on my eye only. This is a retinal scan, identification through biometrics. It has to be done because it is my first time on the base. The system cannot be fooled, your data cannot be falsified. A document can be counterfeited, your eye patterns cannot. This is real life, not the world of the film *Gattaca*. But every security system, no matter how sophisticated, has its weak points. The weak points are always human.

The LoA means that I must be given entry to the base. Because I don't have a military ID card, the guards want me to leave my passport with them. However, I need the passport for entrance to on-base facilities. The contradiction means a higher authority must be called. An American contractor carrying a holstered .45 soon arrives in a few minutes. It occurs to me that he would not find an Iraqi visa in my passport. This is probably a good thing—he would probably conclude that I arrived on a military flight, since U.S. military personnel coming to Iraq do not need visas.

He looks at my LoA and asks me where I'm from. We chat a bit, he asks why I don't have a military ID. I tell him that they were so rushed to get me here that there wasn't time. He chuckles—apparently that is standard operating procedure. Satisfied that I am not an Iraqi insurgent he tells the Africans to let us through.

We walk through the last door onto the base. Before us is a roundabout distributing traffic in several directions. There is a wooden box on a pole holding medical equipment and a concrete "duck

Forward Operating Base Union III

and cover" shelter in case of incoming rockets. On the right side there is a parking lot with a "No Parking" sign hanging from a chain. In the courtyard leading to a building there are more of the rectangular structures. The reason why parking is not permitted is because the lot is full of shipping containers stacked two high. Another building has an ornate porte cochère, housing houses offices on either side of the road beneath an Islamic dome.

The PX, or post exchange, is in a larger, corrugated metal building. The *Stars and Stripes* military newspaper is in a bin outside. Along the bin are racks for backpacks or bags. Backpacks are not permitted inside, not because of fears of retail theft, but because of fears they might contain explosives.

I am excited to see a standard blue U.S. post box. This one has been modified. The drawer had been placed with a bolted-on block of wood with a thin slit so packages cannot be dropped in. Nothing thicker than a #10 envelope could be deposited. Packages might contain bombs.

The last time I sent out office mail it was by Fedex to Germany, where the letters were placed in the German mail. Access to the U.S. mail system should make the office run more smoothly.

Three more Africans guard the entrance to the PX. There is one last I.D. check before we can enter. A facility so well-guarded must house the treasures of Midas. We enter to disappointment. My first thought after so many checks was, "this is it?" Inside was the size of a small convenience store in the States. I thought I would ask someone if this was the only PX on the base, but I didn't say anything. Expecting to find a cornucopia of American goods, I was disappointed with their meager supplies. There weren't even any Milky Way candy bars. Still, the excitement over seeing the mailbox made up for my disappointment.

On the way out near the cashiers there were black footlockers just like the ones I kept in my house on 46th Street. There was a sign saying that the footlockers met U.S. mailing requirements. The PX carried backpacks and flip-flops but no shoes. There were pregnancy test kits. Blank DVD's, USB sticks. Pringles potato chips, bed sheets and pillows. There was one drip coffee maker. Perhaps I will return tomorrow to buy it. There were boxes of Diet Coke as well as basic office supplies, plastic files and containers. There were cleaning supplies, and few tourist items, such as coffee mugs and stuffed toy camels.

I bought a bottle of Clorox bleach to deal with the rat problem in the Sabre Compound. U.S. coins were scarce, so to make change they handed out colored cardboard discs instead of pennies, nickels, dimes and quarters. These printed discs had AAFES printed on them and were only good for use at

AAFES facilities. The total for my purchases was $9.38. After all that.

Coming back outside to the 115 (46° C) degree heat, I walked around to see what other facilities might be available nearby. I was hoping to find the post office, but it was not around. I was told that the post office is behind Building 5, but that information was meaningless. There were no signs showing how to get to Building 5 and my Iraqi companions didn't know how to find it. This base was my place, not theirs.

There was a Popeye's Chicken and a Western Union office with flyers explaining their rules and an offer for Western Union credit cards. There was some kind of coffee shop with real coffee. I wanted to have a cup, but Ahmed is fasting for Ramadan so I didn't think it would be fair for me to drink in front of him. Afterwards we followed the bread crumbs back through the maze and left Forward Operating Base Liberty III. In the cafeteria some of the Iraqis say they are fasting, but I have been behind them in the food line watching them fill their plates during the day. Food here is gratis. The Iraqi Christians at least have an excuse, but not all the Iraqis are Christian.

★★★

Maybe there really is a balance in life. Yesterday

was such a bad day, but today was exciting. Thank God for small pleasures.

A few days ago I wrote a memorandum. Florian sent it back with additions, writing, "be sure to leave this in, exactly as I wrote it." I did so. Today he wrote back complaining that what he wrote is "too generic." I could only point out that these were the words he wanted.

The issue is a common one in the Middle East. A foreign manufacturer wants to replace a local distributor. To do so would require compensating the local agent for goodwill built up during the period of the agency. This is when the foreign manufacturers, desperate not to pay what will be an inflated amount determined by a local court based on figures plucked from the air, will try anything to avoid the local laws.

Ahmed came into the office today. He comes into the office no more than once a week. It's an exaggeration to say he's working here.

They tested the fire alarm today. It sounds nothing like the alarm that sounds when there is an explosion. Today I also received two Fedex packages. The first was a small Fedex box I had sent to myself before leaving. It contained a few books including a legal forms book. This was sorely needed given the lack of available legal precedents at the firm. But now that I have military postal access, I can get books easily at low cost.

The second package contained the typewriter I bought on E-bay, sent from England. Now I have most of the tools I need. Today is simply a great day. I look forward to the future.

Company Formation

SETTING UP A COMPANY in the United States is very easy compared to what is required in the Middle East and in many other countries. A company in the United States can be organized over the phone or by e-mail. The Articles of Incorporation are always standard and there are commercial filing agencies happy to handle all the necessary paperwork and even provide a local address if required. Even the Internal Revenue Service is happy to provide the new company with a tax identification number over the phone so taxes can be properly credited.

In the Middle East, corporate formations consists of meetings a complex set of changing requirements and is usually an exercise in frustration. The requirements are a moving target due to policy considerations and seemingly change from day to day and from official to official.

In the summer of 2010, formation of new companies in Iraq was taking on average ninety days. Of course there were exceptions. Unlike in other countries, every company that wished to establish itself in Iraq needed a security clearance. This was a new and separate requirement over and above all of the other formalities required to establish a business. Cost of incorporation could range from a low of $10,000 to a high of $70,000 or more if there was a problem with the security license. These were competitive rates. Corporate formation in Saudi Arabia will normally run at least $50,000 even though there is no formal security license requirement. The Saudis conduct their security inquiry when employees apply for visas.

Unfortunately, for a company wishing to do business, and perhaps one with a promised contract or even a contract in hand, ninety days is an eternity.

A French catering company had contracts to set up kitchens at work camps for oil companies in remote locations. They were desperate to get started. There was constant pressure to push corporate formations along, and of course this required a good deal of client hand-holding and relying on Ahmed to make the visits the relevant ministries. When Ahmed was working he was very, very good. The problem is that he would disappear for days at a time, I would not hear from him and then there would be nothing to tell the client. "Nothing new" is simply not an acceptable answer when a foreign company asks after the status of their case.

A company wishing to set-up for business in a new jurisdiction will want to know the amount of tax exposure in advance. Unfortunately, this is not always an easy question to answer. In Saudi Arabia, attorneys are forbidden from giving tax advice. Accounting firms compete with law firms for corporate formation business and are quite competitive because of their lower cost structures and superior knowledge of tax law. Fortunately in Iraq there is no such prohibition and so I could answer clients' questions after educating myself about tax matters.

Perhaps because the Coalition Provisional Authority lowered taxes, successive governments have maintained the lower CPA corporate tax rate of a maximum of 15%. Oil sector taxes are set at a maximum of 35%. Curiously, taxation in Iraq often depends on negotiations with the tax authorities. This is especially true where there are benefits to be calculated under foreign investment laws. Foreign companies working on development projects and their foreign employees are exempt from Iraqi income tax.

The CPA in 2004 also imposed a 5% duty on all imports to help pay for the reconstruction of Iraq. Though this levy was abolished by the new customs law, the 5% duty continues to be assessed anyway.

No one knows if taxes paid to the government in Kurdistan will offset taxes owed to the central government. Erbil says yes; Baghdad says no. What Kurdistan really wants is a separate country and it is anyone's guess if they will get it.

The full extent of Kurdish autonomy within the federal republic is still being tested. While the oil industry has been the most visible area of this conflict, it is not the only one. Iraqi Kurdistan has its own customs controls. Commercial agents and insurance agents may obtain an Iraqi Kurdistan registration without being registered in the rest of the Iraq.

Companies may be established in Iraqi Kurdistan without obtaining a commercial registration in the rest of Iraq. Until recently, the amendments to the Companies Law affected by CPA Order No. 64 allowing 100% foreign ownership were not applied in Kurdistan. As a result, foreign investors were not able to hold more than 49% of the shares in companies established in Iraqi Kurdistan.

Slowly the authorities in Kurdistan are abandoning this position, and have started to apply the general Iraqi Companies Law as amended by CPA Order No. 64 of 2004, and Ministerial Instruction No. 196/2004. As a result, the establishment of companies in Kurdistan follows the same rules as the establishment of a company in other parts of Iraq.

In theory we have an office in Erbil. This is, at least, what we have proudly told clients and repeated to ourselves. I received a telephone call today from a client who was in Erbil asking for a meeting tomorrow at our offices there. Because of the security situation, there was no way I could get there and the attorney staffing the Erbil office was not to be found. The reason he could not be found is because he didn't really exist. The Erbil office was yet another virtual office. We had a place where we could meet with a client, but no way to get there. The attorney who afforded us this courtesy spoke Arabic only, so it made no sense to send an English-speaking Japanese client to meet with him in the absence of a translator. Plus, he wanted to meet with someone from the firm, not merely a friendly colleague.

Similarly, the other Baghdad office was unable to assist. I had no contact with anyone there, if they indeed existed. There was no contact with anyone in the Red Zone except Ahmed, and he never showed up until after 5 p.m. There was no one else to send. Florian told me to make excuses, which I did. I offered to meet with the client in the Green Zone but they had no interest at all in traveling to Baghdad. Erbil is a safe city; Americans are viewed as liberators who freed the Kurds from Saddam's oppression. You can wander the city freely. European airlines have just returned to flying into American-friendly Erbil, but its currently their only Iraqi destination: they want to stay as far away from the shooting in Baghdad as possible.

August 21

Florian called me around noon. He decided that he wants me to submit weekly reports. Fair enough. Somehow I have to come up with a list of permits necessary for building construction. He doesn't have a list and neither do I. Where will I find this? I don't know. Looking at the firm's Iraqi precedent library won't help. It's non-existent. The Red Zone office? Still unreachable. I made a note to ask Ahmed the next time he shows up.

At 10 a.m. there was an attack. I didn't hear anything. There was another one in the afternoon. Two daylight attacks, unusual. It was otherwise a quiet day. Tomorrow I will have to hit the ground running, but it shouldn't be as bad as those few days last week.

The Miami-Dade county government has scheduled a hearing before an administrative body called the Value Adjustment Board concerning the price of my home on 46th Street. I need to attend. I sent an email to a lawyer in Miami to try to get someone to handle the hearing. This is so that property tax is not assessed on the pre-crash value of the property. The United States runs its national educational system based on local property taxes. All sorts of local governments receive a share of these taxes as well. For that reason, property in the United States is expensive to keep. A few hours later I received a quote in almost the same amount as the proposed tax bill. This is no solution. I would normally handle such a matter myself, but I am in Iraq. The Board never bothered to ask before setting the hearing.

Max only has two days left before he has to go back to school. He is swamped and can't complete all the tasks he has to finish before he can go.

August 22

There is no agreement concerning the government and talks between the two opposing parties have collapsed. Ahmed told me that there were six mortar attacks in the Red Zone on Sunday. A friend of Ahmed's was killed by a car bomb. They had checked underneath the chassis, but the bomb was put near the car's center line, beyond the reach of the mirror devices used to check the undercarriage. His friend was a lieutenant in the new Iraqi army. There has also been an uptick in attacks on lawyers and judges. Several have been killed in the past week. The insurgents attack established power and those who represent the law. Ahmed says that he won't be dropping by the office at all this week because of all these troubles.

I visited Forward Operating Base Prosperity. The ostensible reason for the trip was to visit the PX, but I really wanted to just familiarize myself with the base. FOB Prosperity is a little bit farther away than FOB Union and security was slightly more relaxed. As a U.S. citizen with a LoA I wasn't even frisked, though Ahmed was frisked at each of the two pedestrian checkpoints we had to pass. There were multiple camouflaged machine gun nests and a tank guarding the main gate. The camp sits on the grounds of one of Saddam's former palaces. This palace was also bombed during the war and was not repaired. There is a U.S. flag on a flag pole outside the bombed-out palace.

They have had seven years to repair the palaces but have not done so because the fighting never stopped long enough. There were man-made lagoons on the road coming up to the palace. When Saddam was in power a dolphin lived in one of the lagoons. The last gate was so large that it spanned the roadway with two tall arches which permitted semi-trailers to pass through.

I learned that the acronym DFAC stands for "dining facility." Three meals are served each day and DFAC's are restricted to military contractors and active duty personnel. That is the reason why there is no commissary, they do all the cooking for you. In Panama, the military commissary was even more popular than the PX. Many American products were only sold at the commissary. There was no such thing as a "10 items or less line." Shoppers filled their carts, sometimes taking two, so that they could re-sell American goods on the grey market. I wrongly assumed that there would be an active commissary trade in Iraq, but there's not. You have to eat in, take-out isn't allowed and so there is no wholesale contrabanding of American food products.

Even though there are several DFAC's on different bases, barbecue is big in the Green Zone. There are lots of outdoor cooking supplies in the PX though I didn't see any grills. I guess that the soldiers don't get enough to eat at the DFAC. Vitamin powders, supplements and body-building supplies were all on sale and filled an entire wall at the PX. There were military souvenirs, state flags and some artwork depicting Iraqi scenes in a subcontractor's store. There was a Subway sandwich shop and another Western Union office. On the bulletin board there was a notice advertising movies and salsa dancing classes. On the way in there was a 24 hour potable water station. The roads are deserted; there are simply too many checkpoints. Iraqis know that they are not welcome here, and even if they have a good reason to be here, it is still too much of a hassle.

No one makes any effort to rebuild. None. The great palaces were taken as a prize of war. They need the land for the base, but don't particularly need the palace itself. So they wrap a chain link fence around it, declare it off-limits and leave it to rot in the Iraqi sun.

I should be able to get shoes at the Prosperity PX. I still don't know where the APO is. There doesn't seem to be any readily available directory.

August 23

Yesterday evening the sirens went off again. This morning a young man wore a "Under New Management" t-shirt, with a stylized map of the United States. I can't tell if this has anything to do with Iraq or if it's some kind of Obama fanboy t-shirt.

The work situation wasn't good today. Florian called with work that needed to meet deadlines: he needs one assignment done in an hour, another within two. This is not good for the long term but I have to give my mouth shut and take it because he is in charge.

August 24

I was on my way to exercise but when I stood at the top of the stairs I noticed that there was some kind of smoke; I thought it was a sandstorm. There was an unusual smell in the air. The smell was a little bit like the smell after a fire, but different. The smell was cordite. Somewhere there had been an explosion, or several explosions. Smoke drifted over the football field obscuring the view. There had been another attack; this one was close. I didn't even hear the alarms. Maybe this time the sirens just didn't have time to go off.

Today I tried to get my DoD badges but was told that they are no longer issued at Forward Base Prosperity, or even in-theater. They told me that I would have to go to Kuwait, or any military base outside of Iraq.

The largest PX, I learned is at VBC: Victory Base Camp, out by the airport. To get there you have to go through the Red Zone. Going by a two car caravan is the minimum security requirement but Sabre recommends three. This has to be arranged in advance and paid for. So I guess I'm not going anytime soon. In the interim I'm stuck. I can't go anywhere. I am in the compound like I am in a prison. If it wasn't for the fact that I am used to being alone I would go mad.

Max sent me pictures from Miami. Maybe I am torturing myself by looking at these things. I don't know. I keep to myself here, like I was in jail. It is the same.

Boycotting Israel

A GERMAN MULTINATIONAL (DAG) acquired an Israeli company that made solar panels. Could DAG could export their new Israeli solar panels to their markets in the Middle East? My portion of the project was to deal with both Iraq and Saudi Arabia.

When legal systems collide defining what is lawful is not easy. A legal question can be answered in the affirmative under one system and in the negative in the other.

The Israeli boycott was established by the Arab League upon the founding of Israel in 1948. The boycott has three levels. The primary boycott prohibits citizens of Arab League countries from conducting business with the Israeli government or Israeli citizens or companies. The secondary boycott prohibits any business worldwide from doing business with Israel. Companies that do so are blacklisted. The tertiary boycott prohibits any entity in the world from conducting business with a blacklisted company. The boycott, then, has extraterritorial reach.

In 1979, Egypt and Jordan concluded a peace treaty with Israel and abolished anti-boycott legislation. In order to enter into a free trade agreement with the United States, Bahrain had to do so the same, though informally the Bahraini Customs Department refuses entry to Israeli goods. Oman is in the same position as Bahrain. Despite its accession to the World Trade Organization in 2005, Saudi Arabia denies entry to Israeli goods. This is accomplished by a Saudi reservation to the document of accession by which it states that anything in the treaty which violates the customs and traditions of the Kingdom of Saudi Arabia will not be permitted. Trade with Israel is construed to violate those traditions.

American law makes it a crime to obey the Anti-Israel boycott, thus making it a crime to comply with a law whose violation is itself a crime.

It is a crime to obey the law.

In Iraq, the legal basis for the boycott is Regulation No. 31/1976 issued by the Ministry of Foreign Affairs and the instructions issued by the Iraqi Boycott Office. The instructions currently in force have not been published, so Ahmed will have to go to the Boycott Office. Or perhaps he could make a call. That is, if he does anything at all. In any event, I did not get anything in writing from him, but he did say that Iraq would not permit Israeli products, whether fully or partly manufactured in Israel, to enter the country. Whether this is simply Ahmed's opinion, the recognized practice or the official position of the government is not entirely clear. So it looks as if there will be no business opportunities for Israel in Iraq, U.S. presence or not.

I doubt that Ahmed researched the issue and there was no substantiation to show the client if we were asked. While helping a client avoid the boycott is a violation of U.S. law, merely advising the client on the law's legal requirements cannot be. I hope.

August 25

Just trying to get caught up. My to-do list fills an entire page. One item after another. It is essentially crazy.

There were bombings all across Iraq yesterday. 61 people died today in coordinated attacks around Iraq. Most of them were policemen. In Baghdad a suicide truck bomber killed 15 and wounded 56. In Basra, a parked minivan filled with explosives killed 12 people.

They are testing the security services.

We had no briefings in the compound.

We just have to get organized here. How can a German firm be so without organization? It seems that everyone lives and works inside Microsoft's Outlook mail program. I don't know how they do it. I cannot. I hate the program. It's a mess. I can't find e-mails. The search function is a joke. I really want to get APO access. That would make life here so much easier. And I would like to get out, at least for a weekend.

How to Enforce a Foreign Judgment

A CLIENT WANTS to know if an Australian judgment can be enforced in Iraq. It has always been difficult to enforce foreign judgments and arbitral awards in Iraq. This is due to the small number of bilateral or international agreements to which Iraq is a party, the strict Iraqi legal requirements for enforcement, and uneven application of the law by the judiciary.

Foreign judgments are only enforceable in Iraq if issued in countries maintaining bilateral agreements with Iraq that permit the enforcement of foreign judicial awards, or in countries named by Iraqi regulations. For example, Regulation No 29 of 1932 provides for the enforcement of judicial awards issued in Canada, Hong Kong, New Zealand, Malta, and Cyprus. In all other cases, unless the foreign country enforces Iraqi judgments the foreign judgment will not be enforced.

Iraq is a signatory state of the 1983 Riyadh Convention for Judicial Cooperation. According to Article 31 of the Convention, judgments rendered in a member state are enforceable in another member state if they are recognized in that state. The Convention provides that a country may refuse enforcement on public policy grounds and for other specified reasons. Article 37 of the Riyadh Convention requires member states to recognize and enforce arbitral awards issued in other member states in the same manner as judgments of the courts of a member state.

The Iraqi Civil Procedure Code addresses Iraqi arbitration in general, but does not contain provisions relating to foreign arbitral awards. Iraq is not a party to the New York Convention on the Recognition and Enforcement of Foreign Arbitral Awards of 1958, but it has signed a number of bilateral agreements and Arab League conventions regarding the enforcement of arbitral awards, including the Riyadh Convention for Judicial Cooperation of 1983, and the Arab Convention on Commercial Arbitration of 1992.

The Arab Convention on Commercial Arbitration applies to commercial disputes between natural or legal persons, regardless of nationality, that are connected by means of commerce with any contracting government or one of its nationals. Its provisions recognize the right of the parties to a contract to agree on commercial arbitration by the Arab Centre for Commercial Arbitration, either in the contract or in a separate agreement concluded after the dispute has arisen.

While a lawsuit against a U.S. Government contractor could not be entertained by an Iraqi Court between 2003 and January 1, 2009, that is not to say that a claimant was without legal recourse. Depending on the circumstances, an action could be brought against a contractor in another jurisdiction.

United States courts seem reluctant to entertain jurisdiction over contractor cases. In 2009, the 11th Circuit Court of Appeals refused to hear a case involving a KBR contractor killed in Iraq in 2004.

Carmichael v. Kellogg Brown Root Services, Inc., 572 F.3rd 1271 (11th Cir. 2009).

August 26

The attacks continue. Six more people were killed. Here in the Green Zone we are isolated from these things. At work I was told to hold off before continuing any big projects. Perhaps we are going to shut down? This was inconvenient news because I have several large projects I am working on.

The bad thing about working for a small law firm or working for any organization other than a large institution, is that someone is constantly looking over your shoulder. Routine responses are elevated to emergencies requiring close coordination. Smaller institutions are unable to provide much logistical support.

Today I sent a request to the gas company to turn off the gas on 46th Street. I had forgotten to do this before I left. Despite all the problems with the Valuation Board, there are two offers on the house. This is good news, I just want out.

I am still exercising, one half hour per day. No heavy lifting. I spend one half hour every day exercising on the treadmill at a speed of 5-6 kph.

August 27

Today I have to get caught up on all of the tasks I have fallen behind on. I have to be smiling and friendly. Sabre confirmed yesterday that I cannot get my initial badge in Iraq. I will have to go to Kuwait. I have to make a list and stick to it and simply knock off the items. Forget that today is my day off.

At the compound, the mercenaries from Uganda and Nepal seem to get along well. They keep to themselves. Their officers are British.

August 28

It has been a few days since there were any sirens.

Going through business cards, I noticed that Bernhard Dolinek's business card lists an APO address. Maybe this is a general military mail address that was assigned to Sabre and I can use it. My inbound mail problems would be over.

August 29

There were two sirens this evening. Around 10 p.m. the second went off and I heard an explosion. It wasn't far away. I could feel the impact.

I asked at Ops about the APO address on Bernhard's business card but no one knew anything. I will get to the bottom of this yet. The Navy is in charge of incoming mail. This is a little strange considering how far we are from the sea. Contractors handle outgoing mail. One of the guys in Ops told me that he thought Dolinek's address was the same one as the German Embassy. This is unlikely; Bernhard is not a diplomat.

I think I'll trade in the truck I left in Atlanta for a car and leave it in Chicago to use during occasional visits. At the moment, I am living out of my suitcases in a glorified college dorm room in the Green Zone.

August 30

Vice-President Joe Biden came to the Green Zone today, unannounced. He snuck in on a C-17 cargo plane and met with government leaders. Perhaps that might explain why there were two attacks this evening. I felt one of them. It was close. What could they be aiming at? If I know Biden was here, so do the insurgents. When Biden can arrive during the day and not sneak in like he is ashamed then this war will truly be over. Round II of the war is over, that is all. In Round III they will be flying the helicopters off the roof of the embassy. It will not be pretty.

Ahmed sends word that he will be hospitalized for a week because of a kidney stone. During this time he will not be coming to the office. My guess is that his recuperation period will be lengthy and all of it spent away from the office. He should be careful though—if medical excuses escalate too much you are ultimately painted into the corner of having to fake your own death. Even Ferris Bueller realized that at some point he would have to pretend to cough up a lung to get out of class.

There was a lot of work today—I had to write a memo for Exxon on Iraqi construction and environmental permitting. Another client wanted a comprehensive list of all the permits necessary to commence business in Saudi Arabia. Trying to come up with an accurate number is trying to hit a moving target—the list is determined not only by the type of business, but its location and how aggressive certain ministries might be at any given moment. All you can do is make a rough estimate, unless you are visiting the ministries on a daily basis. Many firms do this, but we do not have our own office in Saudi Arabia and I am not told the type of business that our client will be exploring.

Obtaining Local Permits

THE ISSUE OF PERMITTING, that is, advising on the permits that are required to set up business in Iraq, is one of keen interest to our clients and one that occupies a good deal of my time. Unfortu-

Obtaining Local Permits 129

nately, there is no single source where this information can be obtained. Listing all the steps required for a construction project is not a trivial or even a precise exercise.

The regulatory environment in Iraq is complex. A single project may require permitting by dozens of different agencies operating in a changing legal environment. Determining what laws apply or are being applied was always a challenge.

For example, the Municipalities Administration Law (Law No.13 of 2001) authorizes Baghdad's Director General to impose fines on contractors who build without a license. The Ministry of Planning has adopted the European FIDIC construction standards. There are no local building codes in Iraq. Site development laws all predate the overthrow of the prewar regime.

No general permit is required for a site built as required by a government contract. Both the Civil Aviation Authority and the Ministry of Transportation are involved if there is going to be a helipad or planes flying in and out of the facility, such as in a remote camp. Medical facilities have to be approved by the Public Clinics Department at the Ministry of Health. Proposed technical specifications have to be submitted. A license for medical waste handling and disposal must also be obtained.

If you think you can avoid involving the Ministry of Health by simply not building health facilities think again: occupational safety and health rules and the Labor Law require basic health care facilities if there are at least fifty employees on site. Companies employing one hundred or more workers must hire a physician or contract for medical services. Medicine and medical care for employees must be provided free of charge.

The Ministry of Communications weighs in if communications towers or microwave platforms are needed. The local municipal office must also grant a permit. They will not touch your paperwork unless you submit six copies along with your original, which by the way, does not go to the technical staff but instead to the legal department in order to make sure that the formal application requirements are met. If not, all seven copies get sent back.

If the application is compliant, the legal department then advises the technical department, which has a look-see. If the technical department feels that the application meets municipal requirements, the application is sent to the Ministry of Industry and Minerals for preliminary approval and issuance of the building permit. The municipal government's planning and follow-up department reviews and presumably, follows-up. Once the preliminary building permit is issued, the developer has to pay a fee for building inspection and the connection of utilities.

But don't start to dig yet. Before turning a spade you need approvals from the Iraqi Telecommunications and Post Company as well as the Ministry of Electricity. These agencies will be happy to inspect the project area, though completing these inspections has been known to "exceed the period prescribed by law." Get ready to wait.

The Iraqi government controls the supply of water but if you want to sink your own well you will need a permit. Because of overlapping jurisdictions, three agencies are involved: the Ministry of Irrigation, the Ministry of Environment and the Ministry of Health all have a say before you turn your first shovelful of earth in the hopes of supplying water.

Before the invasion, the Ministry of Electricity was responsible for regulating electric utilities. During the invasion, the grid was destroyed. Metal vendors vandalized junction boxes, pole pots and anything else they could get their hands on. So the private sector was forced to use private generators. These generators were supposed to be registered with the local notary having jurisdiction over the area in accordance with Law No. 7 of 1999 ("Machine Registration"). If your generator is used, you have to provide the names of all previous owners. Meeting these requirements in a war zone is an exercise in futility and so they were ignored. Nevertheless, the requirements are still on the books.

If, miraculously, there is state-provided power in your area, you must have an inspection to determine how much you will be charged due to the project's impact on the existing power structure. And you need a copy of an electric bill from someone nearby. It's not sufficient to ask the Ministry for your neighbor's electric bills—you have to somehow obtain them on your own. You should hope for neighbors who are friendly and the absence of any competitors. Payment of electric bills in Iraq is not accomplished through direct deposit or via the mails. Instead, a bill collector will come by to pick up your payment.

Light poles cannot be installed at random. A plan of the area showing proposed placement must be submitted and the appropriate fee will be calculated according to the dimensions of the pole.

In other areas, regulation is less comprehensive. No special license is required for the transportation of hazardous materials. Nor are there any general safety laws or regulations in effect. Despite the absence of regulation, inspectors from the Ministry of the Environment will come to inspect anyway. But be careful: in theory environmental inspectors exist only on paper. The "Environmental Protection and Improvement Law," Law 27 of 2009, provided for them. Unfortunately, inspectors have yet to be appointed under that 2009 law.

Firefighting and safety is the responsibility of the Civil Defense Department of the Ministry of the Interior. Civil Defense inspectors are similarly sure to make a visit to the project site.

Obtaining Local Permits 133

The division of functions between all these agencies at the national, regional, and local levels is not entirely clear largely because the Iraqi regulatory system is still in transition. This means that anything can happen. In theory environmental impact statements are required. In practice, no one may ask for them. The Hydrocarbons Law will impact environmental issues and oilfield services, but this law, perhaps the one the West is most interested in, is still in draft form only.

★★

Iraq still has no government, nor does it appear likely that it will get one. In the absence of a government there is a power vacuum and the violence will increase.

I haven't finished my time sheets, they must be finished. I am still having a lot of difficulties with the firm's computer systems. I cannot enter data into the cells on the on-line spreadsheet. They try to walk me through their system but we cannot figure out why it is not working. Three hours later I figure out the issue: numbers need to be between quotation marks before they can be entered into cells on the spreadsheet. The spreadsheet was expecting German-style quotation marks and rejected English, French, Spanish, Italian, Norwegian, Swedish, etc. quotation. I was just as unfamiliar with their conventions as they are with mine. Our frames of reference are different and that is why we could not find the answer to the problem. When I use German-style quotation marks the spreadsheet accepts the data without question.

There were several problems of this nature. Florian asked me for a photograph for the firm website, so I sent him a typical headshot. Almost immediately I was told that the photograph wasn't acceptable. This was odd, so I asked why? Was the dpi wrong? Was it RGB color where they needed CMYK? No, it was none of these. They needed a 2/3rds body shot; the "standard" for German web pages. I told him sorry, I only had the "standard" for North American-and for that matter, Middle Eastern web pages. So he asked me if I couldn't hire a photographer and get a new photograph taken.

In Baghdad.

In the Green Zone.

Sure.

Come to think of it, I don't think my picture ever did get posted on the firm's web site.

I was supposed to have a meeting the day after tomorrow in the Red Zone but Ops says it is simply too dangerous for me to go by myself. I need an armed escort of either Nepalese or the British soldiers. The cost to the firm would be in excess of $1500, so I tell the clients that they will have to come to me.

It's confirmed that I am going to Germany on September 6th for a week. Hopefully I'll be able to get my military ID's there. What would be great would be a side trip to Spain, but I don't believe that this will be possible.

I am worried about Max. He started school today. His academic schedule seems to be quite heavy. But that was the whole point, right? "You might as well go to Saudi Arabia because I have to finish school."

August 31

Another attack. This one came around 4:30 in the afternoon. I felt this one as well. I assume it was in honor of Biden's visit. In the evenings, I heard machine gun fire and then helicopters quickly appeared overhead, chasing the source.

Today was officially the last day of U.S. military combat operations. They say that U.S. forces are here now only in the role of military advisors: the war is over. No one really believes that.

Meanwhile, the rounds are getting closer.

On the 6th of September I should be going to Berlin. I have to make my way to a military base somewhere, but I don't know where to go. Perhaps

I'll have to go to England. If I can get my ID's and if I can get APO access, things here won't be so bad.

The funny part is that it's not Al-Qaeda or the mortar rounds that cause all the stress. Sure, you jump when you hear the explosions or when the sirens go off, but what really gets to me is the stress from work, unreasonable deadlines, no precedents, having to do the most simple things from scratch and then having everything you do questioned by people who are safe and miles away.

In the late afternoon the computer was running very slowly because I was running an OCR program. This was a hack to make up for the lack of secretarial support. But running a processor-intensive task like OCR on an older laptop with limited memory was an iffy proposition. If I could OCR a short text in Arabic I could pop it into Google translate to at least get an idea of what the text was about. Google's translations were far from perfect, but they were getting better. Otherwise translation means a delay of several days and maybe several weeks. It simply is too expensive to translate everything. There are already enough delays. Today was one phone call after another. And tomorrow is Wednesday, the penultimate day of the week and usually one of the busiest days.

Exercise has kept me going. Just like in prison. When I don't work out it feels like the day is really missing something. Today I couldn't exercise because of a postponed telephone conversation with a Fulbright and Jaworski lawyer in Dubai. The first thing I'll do in Berlin is take a long hot shower. The Navy calls these "Hollywood" showers, where the water is permitted to run and run.

The only issue is the house. And the Tuduj case. Iraq makes it impossible to do much about either.

I am exhausted.

September

September 1

A STRESSFUL DAY. I was working on the Big Oil Company memo all day. Florian disagrees with the conclusions. We are working without a net, without any basis for our opinions. It is very difficult to get guidance from the ministries and Ahmed hasn't yet surfaced from his latest absence. There is no backup. Our Iraqi law library is almost non-existent. I use the United Nations texts; they are good but a little dated. Especially in this environment I need recent material. The law changes daily, and clients want the latest advice from the ministries; they want to know if prewar rules will apply or if the government is going to issue new regulations.

The questions clients ask require parsing the law and providing answers which have policy consequences in a vacuum. Because their questions are analyzed without stakeholder input, it is impossible to determine whether the ministry that has jurisdiction will necessarily agree with our analysis. If another ministry objects, the assent obtained will disappear. Unless the ministry issues a formal directive, no one will admit that there was ever informal concurrence in the first place. For this reason, it is impossible to give good, reliable answers and without a real government no one wants to stick their neck out by making a decision or issuing guidance. The oil companies want to make deals with the regional government in Erbil directly but the central government threatens to void any such agreement and take commercial reprisals against any company that would dare strike such a regional bargain.

At 4:30 in the afternoon there was another close-by explosion. I felt it. A kilometer away, maybe less. Daylight attacks are increasing. Just like the movie *Aliens,* usually they come at night. They almost always come at night.

Around 10 p.m. there were sirens, but this time I didn't hear any explosions.

September. 2

I am definitely going to Berlin. Ahmed called to say that he has to go to Amman for kidney stone surgery. The recuperation period is indefinite, so he does not know when he will be back. Not that he was ever in the office on a regular basis anyway. I am flying Middle Eastern Airways to Beirut and then on to Berlin. With Ahmed formally out of commission I can't be away that long. There will be no on to cover the office. My Red Zone colleagues, if they exist, have never shown up here. In a way, I really shouldn't go to Germany at all. I've become accustomed to my prison here. It's comfortable, like an old folk's home.

This afternoon I went to the credentials office at Camp Prosperity. The visit cut short. Because they no longer issue credentials, called a CAAC card, in Iraq, they referred me to other Department of Defense installations in Germany where I can get my credentials. With the CAAC card I will have easy access to all DoD facilities.

I was able to find the post office and could mail a few letters. The post office is a double-wide trailer sitting on a wooden platform. Built-up wooden steps lead to the entrance. One of the doors had a wooden slot for letters—but I went inside anyway. They took the letters but didn't hand-cancel them in front of me. Still for less than fifty cents each the letters are on their way.

Work is oppressive. Florian says I'm taking too long with my memos, though he has no problem interrupting the workflow. Sometimes these tasks need uninterrupted thought. How am I supposed to get the work done? I am office manager, receptionist, secretary and paralegal. Not that I mind, but performing all of these other duties slows some of the others down. To get caught up I will have to work through the weekend. That's OK, but I have a feeling that I am going to be fired. I am expendable. The only reason that they keep me is because I am willing to undergo the attacks and they can't get anyone else.

Florian called me at 1930 and I ended up working till 2200. I will have no weekend.

September 3

There were no sirens today. I went to the pharmacy on foot. U.S. Lipitor was $55, the Indian-made generic $15. This is one of the advantages of living overseas. I guess I should get medical insurance.

I sent Amir a message on MENA's internal e-mail system only to have it bounce back reporting an unknown address. I sent messages to the head office in Munich asking to check up on the problem, but there was no response. An hour or two later Florian sent a message to advise that Amir had been let go. When I asked why, I was told it was because he had "insulted" Ahmed. Ahmed did not look like the kind of guy who would be bothered by an injudicious comment. I was disappointed to lose Amir. Amir was a helpful, competent lawyer who made a substantial contribution to the Green Zone office. Even though he was far away, he made a difference. Without him things would be more difficult.

I took this episode as a warning—Ahmed was untouchable. I resolved to have as little to do with him as possible. Florian wasn't making my job any easier.

September 4

No sirens today. Once again, Florian was upset with a memo I wrote. This was the anti-corruption memo for the Big Chemical Company. I know he's not going to to like the Foreign Corrupt Practices Act memorandum either. I have an all-day meeting tomorrow. Everyone else seems happy with my work except for him.

I have my ticket, I leave on Monday for Berlin. The flight leaves Baghdad at 3:00 p.m. but after connecting in Beirut doesn't arrive in Berlin until late evening. I have to pack everything up. The room must be empty in case someone wants to use it during my absence, or in case I don't come back. Tomorrow there is an all-day meeting schedule but the arrangements have not been finalized. Around 0700 they will start calling, six hours from now.

Today I was supposed to get my timesheets up to date and finish the Big Oil Company memo. I finished the memo but didn't even get to the timesheets. Meanwhile, I was sent another document to review. If you let people walk all over you, they will.

There were no sirens today. The meeting I have to go to is in the Red Zone and there is no security for me. Security can't be arranged. Red Zone trips require 72 hours' notice. I had no idea. There was what, ten e-mails on the subject? Twelve? I had to pull teeth to get any information from the client. This is yet another example of no support from the home office. No one knows about the requirements until they are stated too late and afterwards there are complaints that no one was ever advised of their existence. There are no instruction or orientation manuals to read. You don't know what you're supposed to know until it's too late.

When I arrived in the Green Zone I slept in my clothes so that I could leave the room quickly in case of an attack. I don't sleep in my clothes anymore nor do I hit the floor when the sirens warn of incoming shells. I was a little concerned when I walked to the pharmacy last night, but otherwise I am pretty blasé about the security issue.

September 5

Today was the closest strike yet. Less than a kilometer away, maybe 500 meters. No one knows if it was a mortar, a rocket or even a suicide bomber. Whatever it was, we felt it. The general consensus is that it was a mortar. Suicide bombers target crowds, places where there are a lot of people. Not compounds with blast walls. There is nothing in the area of the explosion. I was standing by the window making tea when I heard it; the windows rattled.

Afterwards, I went to talk with Tony from Operations. Eyad and Lynne, two Iraqi Christians from Ops, were there. No one was sure what the insurgents were targeting, since the U.S. Embassy lies in the other direction. Perhaps they are trying to get the range right. Eyad thought that the bomber had been caught and then blew himself up at a checkpoint. No one really knows for sure. I could see a plume of greyish-white smoke in the distance. That was the second siren this morning.

The first siren coincided with the arrival of a delegation from Korea. Welcome to the Green Zone, ladies and gentlemen. There was a ridiculous show on the BBC titled, "After the War" selling the idea that the war is over. This simply is not true.

I don't know what's happening at the office. I spent the rest of the afternoon on time sheets. They always take up more time than they should. I don't know if the problem is one of language or data entry. Florian had another mean comment again today. I can't take this looking over your shoulder supervision. Nothing will get done. I am flying to Berlin tomorrow. I can use the days off, but I have a feeling that there won't be any days off. Perhaps I will have some peace on the airplane.

R & R

September 6

AT 0700, THE SIRENS went off. I heard no explosions. A great way to start the day. I had strange dreams but don't remember them. Perhaps because the problems they address are not solvable.

Today I fly to Beirut and then on to Berlin. I have to deal with office harassment for only three more hours.

Living in this place is seeing my past and my future at once. My past is a college dorm, my future is the Little Sisters of the Poor Home for the Aged.

If I look back on the past month it has been very productive. I've even lost weight.

There are a few loose ends, bills that I have to pay. The house on 46th Street. The pick-up truck.

I was supposed to leave at 1 p.m. At ten minutes to one, I walked into Ops. The theater-size telescreen displays a map of Baghdad. There are colored dots on the map. Below, a scrolling legend identifies the dots. An IED, exploded or not, SAF, small arms fire, a mortar attack. Clayton told me that yesterday there was an incident in the Red Zone at Iraqi

Army headquarters. A suicide bomber covered by a sniper blew himself up at a checkpoint. When the medics came to collect the dead, a sniper started firing and a two man team entered the base with automatic weapons, throwing grenades and killing Columbine-style as they went from floor to floor. U.S. troops at headquarters engaged; so much for "advisory force" only. The Iraqi military strangely told the U.S. forces to stop; but by then they had already killed one of the insurgents. The other was surrounded and Iraqi troops moved in. Then he blew himself up.

Over 25 were killed in the episode, six days after the U.S. announced the end of military operations. This is the second attack on Iraqi military headquarters this month.

Clayton's phone rang and I heard him say, "he's right here, he's coming down." I walked down the corrugated iron plankway on the side of the second floor of the building to a stairway. I walked down and over to the patio by the cafeteria where I was met by Georgie. Georgie is a British mercenary, mid-40's. He gave me my security briefing.

There would be three cars. The scout vehicle would usually lead, but not always. I would have my body armor and helmet if I wanted to wear them. It would be best not to tell me all the things that could happen because they had already happened to others. If I could follow directions that would be enough.

He said there were too many scenarios and he didn't want to scare me. I would be riding in the back seat. If he said "DOWN DOWN DOWN" I was to drop to the floor of the car. The vehicle would be armored. Ops would monitor our progress along the way by radio and satellite positioning. "Are we OK?" he asked. "We're OK," I answered. I can follow orders.

I pulled my bag and carried my briefcase to the compound entrance. Past the door I could see an armored Toyota Land Runner. The engine was running and the door was open for me. An Iraqi guard held the body armor and a helmet for me to put on. They open the door for you because it is so heavy that some people, not accustomed to the extra weight, lose their balance, fall and are injured.

My bags were put in the scout car by the Iraqi guard who shut the Land Runner's door after me. There were two men in the car, Georgie and the Iraqi who didn't give his name. The gate to the compound closed behind us after we backed up and pulled out. We drove to the end of the street and turned right toward the main road; reaching the Four Soldiers roundabout we changed direction and turned into a road with blast walls on either side. We passed an Iraqi traffic checkpoint and then we merged with Iraqi traffic coming from the Red Zone.

Georgie sat in the passenger seat while his Iraqi colleague drove. Each of them had a fully-loaded automatic weapon next to them. Full auto really isn't that useful; you empty the magazine too quickly and then unless you have another at hand your only defense is to make a clicking sound. Fortunately full auto can be turned off.

At the last checkpoint there was a tank on the left side of the road with its turret pointed at the traffic ahead. A sign warned drivers of military vehicles to raise their weapons to their highest elevation before entering traffic. The sign depicted an armored car with its mounted machine gun pointing to the sky.

Georgie would report to Ops if there was anything at all out of the ordinary. A vehicle broken down on the side of the road and even a woman walking nearby merited a report as well. He called to advise the scout car that a vehicle was approaching from the rear at high velocity and after the vehicle overtook us, he reported that fact as well.

We soon came upon a checkpoint. We pulled over as a five car convoy formed in front of us. There were only two lanes. First an armored vehicle with a turret entered the blast wall lane followed by a three car convoy like ours. But before we reached that lane, another armored car pulled in front of us.

They sped off while we were held at the checkpoint. Georgie reported all of this on the radio.

To our right there was a line of Iraqi vehicles waiting to go through the checkpoint. The left lane was for vehicles with military credentials. As so often happens, when there is a long line of cars some of the drivers will pull out of the line to see if there is another way around. There wasn't. There was only our authorized vehicle lane and the Iraqi drivers knew that without military credentials they should not enter. Cars quickly filled the gap that the exiting driver left, preventing him from getting back into the line and blocking traffic.

As we passed the checkpoint Georgie and his Iraqi sidekick opened their doors and raised their ID's above the roof of the car. You can't roll the window down in an armored car. The sign said, "100% ID check" but no one asked me for any identification: I was the client, the passenger, the cargo. There was a brief exchange of greetings in Arabic and we were waived through. Near the watchtowers signs in English read, "No stopping for any reason. If you stop, you may be fired upon." Not a good place to break down. We did not stop.

★★★

When the invasion started, the airport was one of the first targets captured. Now, the airport is under joint Iraqi-U.S. jurisdiction. As we approached the airport, a sign commanded us to turn off all electronic counter-measures. Roadside bombs are often activated by cell phones, specialized thick cylindrical antennas are placed on top of military and security vehicles in order to block cellphone transmissions. "At least, that's the idea," Georgie said.

We entered another lane between two blast walls. There we had to stop so that our vehicles and luggage could be checked by an explosives-detecting dog. The dog was a German shepherd, its handler seemed to be American. I didn't get out of the vehicle, but Georgie and his aide did. There was a towel over Georgie's gun, but he removed it so the handler could see the weapon.

While Georgie and his sidekick were out of the car, I waited. We were given the go-ahead and then proceeded to the airport terminal. There were fewer cars on this access road. We pulled up to the Departures area. I said goodbye and got out of the car but Georgie told me that the job wasn't over. Georgie said goodbye and said that his Scottish colleague in the scout car would be taking me to the airline gate on foot.

There was an Iraqi security checkpoint where I was frisked. I was instructed to walk past the X-ray station. About thirty feet away my bags were placed on the concrete and another dog and its handler appeared. After the dog showed no interest in my bags, we were permitted to proceed. Through all of this, we were still outside the terminal building.

We reached the terminal entrance doors and a guard asked for my passport and then asked where I was going and on what airline. The guards then put my bags through an X-ray machine. I said goodbye to the Sabre Security detail and they pointed me towards the next set of X-ray machines, no more than 25 meters away from the first set.

I presented my ticket at the Middle Eastern Airways line. There were Ugandan soldiers repacking suitcases while arguing about excessive baggage charges and per-piece weight limitations. They were taking small appliances back to Africa. One had a microwave, which was out of its box and on the floor in the line; the other had a DVD player. Though there were only three or four of them, the scene was chaotic. Airline staff processed my ticket and pointed me towards Immigration. I showed my passport to the officers there. We had a brief conversation while they checked for my exit permit, took my picture and stamped my passport. There would be two more X-Ray examinations before I was permitted to board the plane.

One hour later, MEA 323, an Airbus 320, took off for Beirut.

This is why going away for the weekend really isn't an option.

The airport in Beirut had been bombed by Israelis in 2006; it sits in a valley between two Shi'a villages on surrounding mountains. Those of us who didn't have Lebanese passports or who were in transit were taken into the basement and passed through immigration. The officer seemed upset that I did not have a visa for Lebanon. I had several hours to kill before leaving for Berlin. Perhaps he was worried that I might try to stay and claim refugee status if MEA was unable to fly to Berlin.

I walked all around the airport. There was a Virgin Records store where I picked up a DVD of Lebanese short films and a copy of *The Girls of Riyadh,* a best-selling novel by a Saudi writer that had just been translated into English. The religious authorities in Saudi Arabia had tried to ban the novel and had stormed the Riyadh Book Fair in an effort to do so, but the Saudi labor minister extended his protection to the author by praising her book and the religious police backed off. I started reading it while the sun set. By the time we reached Berlin, I still hadn't finished.

Berlin

MIDDLE EASTERN AIRLINES didn't fly to Berlin's main airport, Tegel Airport, but instead used the airport for the former German Democratic Republic, Schönefeld. Shönefeld airport was simply not up to the challenge of being the airport for the capital city of Europe's biggest economy. Except for processing the MEA flight, the airport was closed. Two immigration officers handled the passengers and as one or two of the passengers demonstrated some kind of immigration irregularity, things slowed while supervisors were sought. Shops were closed, except for a kiosk selling coffee. My phone didn't work. I removed the Iraqi SIM and replaced it with a U.S. SIM but that didn't work either. I didn't have any Euros to pay for a cab. I tried to get an Internet connection at the kiosk as Florian had promised to e-mail arrival instructions but I could not get on-line.

Berlin hasn't gotten used to its status as united Germany's new capital. Midnight is not terribly late in the overall scheme of things, but currency exchanges were closed and all I had was a 100 euro note. No one would give me change. Nor was it possible to buy a local SIM. Finally I found an ATM and got smaller bills so I could take a taxi. The firm had not arranged for anyone to meet me.

When the plane landed at 1 a.m., the airport was pretty much deserted. All the money exchange bureaus were closed. I had no euro and there was no place to buy them. I was able finally to get 50 euro from an ATM. The firm had made a reservation for me in a hotel well outside the city center. I asked several cab drivers if they had change but the language barrier frustrated these efforts. Finally I found a driver who had change and understood English and we set off towards the hotel.

The cab ride to the Adrema Gold Inn on Gotzkowskystrasse 20 was forty euro. Unfortunately my hotel was not in the Central Business Distict but was on the outskirts of town. To be more precise, it was in the middle of nowhere in a neighborhood that had already gone to sleep. The drive seemed to take forever and wherever we were going, it was away from the city center. I started to become even more concerned when we seemed to be driving into a forest. This turned out to be the Tiergarten park. I later learned that Florian liked to book people in this hotel because it was inexpensive—fair enough, but whatever was saved due to the low rack rate was eaten up by taxi fares to and from the center of town. I later learned that there was a hotel on Friedrichstrasse just a few doors down from the office.

When I arrived at the hotel it was clear that they weren't expecting me. A guard had to open the door. Apparently it is considered bad manners to arrive so late.

They did not have my reservation which was hardly a surprise since Florian often forgot that his ideas cannot come to fruition without execution. I paid for the room and went upstairs. It was now almost four in the morning. I reached my room and finished the Saudi book.

★★★

In the morning I was greeted with a nasty e-mail from Florian. He was upset that no one was in the office in the Green Zone and frustrated that he could not reach me while I was in the air. The fact that I was traveling had slipped his mind and apparently he had forgotten that Ahmed was off somewhere due to his latest medical or other problem.

Florian hated the Big Oil Company memorandum. He demanded that I revise it immediately and questioned out loud whether I should stay with the firm. He complained that the memorandum contained too much of a discussion of American law, though an analysis of the application of the Foreign Corrupt Practices Act was what really concerned the Big Oil Company. One line of the memorandum

I had written stated that "the regulated are prohibited from giving anything of value to the regulator." Florian said that he did not understand what this meant.

Florian insisted that I meet him in the office at 0900. When I received the email, it was already 1000. I wasn't sure where the office was located. I only had an address. Florian was unconcerned with these technicalities of time and place. The cosmos should conform to his wishes and not the other way around.

I asked the front desk if there were any messages for me but there were none. My phone still did not work. Without a time machine there was no way I was going to make a 9 a.m. meeting. This was typical Florian—set something up in your own mind, take ineffective measures to communicate the unknowable and then bemoan the lack of compliance.

I slowly ate breakfast by myself. It didn't seem that Berlin was going to be a vacation at all. I tried to look up the address of the office on the Internet but could only find references to Munich, Egypt and Dubai. Finally, I called the Munich office and was directed to an address a few doors down from what was once the fulcrum of the Cold War: Checkpoint Charlie.

I sat in the lobby trying to analyze the situation. Obviously I was going to be fired. I could not expect any funds from him. I would have to buy a ticket from Berlin back to Miami. I had left some personal effects in Baghdad, including this diary. These would be lost. I would have to go to the office and confront Florian. Under these circumstances there were two alternatives. The first would be to make a mad dash for the office and hope that Florian would still be there, apologize profusely and make arrangements to return to the United States. Or I could behave like a responsible adult and catch a cab to the office after finishing my coffee. I chose the latter course.

After the expensive taxi ride the night before, I didn't have enough euro left for the taxi ride to the office and the hotel would not change dollars. So I had to search the neighborhood for an ATM. I walked for a few blocks and eventually found a bank. Outside, my tropical weight suit was entirely inappropriate for Berlin. I came back to the hotel and stood outside to try to flag down a taxi. From time to time cabs passed but most either had passengers or were on their way to pick up a pre-arranged fare. Finally a driver stopped and I gave him the address on Friederichstrasse. By day I got a good view of the park I had passed in the evening. While it was extensive, it was hardly a forest. We soon were passing through commercial areas and reached the address. Florian wasn't there and there was no reference to our firm in the building's directory.

There was a sign on the door of Friedrichstrasse

58 with a list of tenants, but none identified Florian or any of his companies as tenants. The address said that the office was on the third floor, but it was impossible to tell just from the names of the companies whether any of them were on the third floor. So I waited until someone came to the door and buzzed a company. I followed her in and went to the third floor.

I told the receptionist that I was looking for Florian and was asked to sit in the waiting room. She left the reception area and a few minutes later returned with another woman who did know Florian but he hadn't been in the office that morning. It wasn't a MENA law office at all—Florian had merely established some kind of a relationship with a group of German consultants and this was their office. There were two empty rooms which we were free to use. If I would like to wait I could do so, but they had no information as to when or even if he was coming. So Florian had made no effort to make the nine o'clock meeting either.

The consultants' business was advising family businesses in the Middle East. I read their advertising materials and waited. After an hour or so, Florian came in, charming, friendly; as if none of the e-mails he had sent the previous day had been sent. About the memo, he said, "don't worry, these are growing pains, we can work through that." And just like that, we were best of friends again.

Florian and I had lunch in a nearby restaurant as if we old friends. He said the problems we were having were normal in an office and we would get through them. I shouldn't worry. He emphasized this by inviting me to Munich to come and meet his family and the team there, though the precise date of the trip was left open. The principal task for the afternoon would be to revise the memorandum and obtain a copy of a report on Iraq that had been prepared by a Washington think tank. I told him that I would have to return to the hotel to check out. There wasn't a good deal of time left in the afternoon, but Florian felt there was enough time to get everything done.

No one had thought to call the think tank and simply ask for a copy of their report. In these Internet days, too many researchers believe that if a document is not on the Internet, it simply does not exist. There are other problems in doing research by telephone. The United States tends to be xenophobic, so foreign accents tend to be viewed with suspicion. The individual who has a copy of the sought-after report may be out of the office, at lunch, on vacation, on leave or simply not answering his phone. It may take several calls to reach the desired person and then and only then can the dance of convincing him to release the document begin.

The downloading wars have convinced everyone that whatever drivel that sits on their desks is valuable intellectual property and worthy of protection. Once upon a time, "can I get a copy?" was an innocuous request. A person sharing a document with you was only doing just that. Now that person must consider whether he would want to share the document with the world, since you are capable of doing so. Answering the question becomes more difficult, "no" is heard more often than not and obtaining a copy of a document is an unrewarded achievement. "Unrewarded" because too many remember the days when documents were simply shared. No longer.

For all of these reasons I favor a two-pronged approach: first a fax or letter explaining who I am, why I need the document, and that I will be calling to make the request. Then I make the promised call. An e-mail request by itself rarely is effective. E-mail is all too easy to ignore and all too often never arrives. E-mail gets caught in spam filters, is subject to domain bans and can disappear in threaded conversations. E-mail works well until it doesn't.

When I began my legal career, like many others I read Jay Foonberg's *How to Start and Build a Law Practice*. Foonberg always recommended sending clients paper. Paper, being physical, must be dealt with physically. Someone must take action, even if that action is to throw the paper away. Physical letters are treated as if their content is more important than the same content contained in an e-mail. So that afternoon I made several phone calls to Washington from Berlin and sent one fax in an effort to get Florian his report.

If I was going to be effective in Baghdad, I needed business cards and getting them printed in the Red Zone was out of the question. Ahmed simply wasn't around enough to get this task done. I decided to have the cards printed in Munich and sent to me in Berlin. Unfortunately, the cards had been sent to the Adrema Gold Inn by regular mail. They finally arrived two days after I checked out. Of course, by that time no one at the hotel remembered me. It must be difficult for the police when they have to chase a criminal who has stayed in a hotel. Strange though—I had given my passport upon check-in and a copy was made. The reception desk doesn't have the ability to refer to these records. Or they simply didn't bother.

Florian asked me to meet him at the China Club that evening, a private club next to the Adlon Hotel. He told me that there was an event that would begin 6 p.m., but as it would be in German, I should plan to arrive near the tail end. I met with several German businessmen; we discussed Iraq, the United States, the war and international relations. Linguistically I was out of it, though I know enough German to say hello and thank you and tell the bartender *wasser bitte*. Speaking a language is a matter of only 1000 words; getting by, even fewer. I found myself breaking into Arabic or even Spanish. I got back at the hotel at midnight.

The next day I moved to the Hotel Gendarm Nouveau, a hotel on Charlottenstrasse 61, near the office and the Gendarmenmarkt. After checking in, I walked back to the office. Florian had already left on the train back to Munich. He left a note with the key codes so that I could get back into the building. The others at the office had no relationship with us at all—they were simply another business that had rented space to Florian. It would have been helpful had he advised me of the nature of this relationship beforehand; it would have made things less bewildering.

I began the day all but without a job; by the end of the day I was feeling secure again. I shouldn't have done so, but I believed Florian's reassurances. With Florian gone the tension was considerably reduced. I had been out of Baghdad for just a day, but now I could rest. I was happy just to be out of Iraq, to feel the cold, to be free of Baghdad's stifling heat. Not to mention the explosions.

I went back to Friedrichstrasse and found a mobile phone shop where I could purchase a SIM card. I gave the office address and telephone number and was online in an instant. I stopped at a bakery and treated myself to a "berliner." In my home town, we called these "bismarks." Strangely, wasps—dozens of them—were flying around inside the display counter where the pastries and bread rolls were kept. No one did anything about them. Berlin is a very clean city, especially coming from Iraq, but the ubiquity of these poisonous insects was disconcerting.

There were no messages from Florian when I got back to the office the next day, and only minor matters to handle from Iraq. It looked like—finally—I would have some free time.

I still had the information sheet from the identification office at FOB Prosperity listing places where I could obtain my CAAC card. One of them was Wiesbaden. I could take a train from Berlin to Frankfurt and then go to the base at Wiesbaden the next day. I told Florian that I would have to go to Frankfurt for a few days. He had assumed, characteristically and without checking, that the cards were issued in Iraq. This is one of the problems of working for a small organization, one without a personnel office. The smaller the office the less likely a particular circumstance could be handled routinely.

I checked out of the hotel and took a taxi to the railway station in Berlin. Unlike Schönefeld, the train station was large and befitting for a country's capital. I purchased a ticket to Frankfurt. The next train left in the early afternoon. The ride was a pleasant one; the train passed the Volkswagen factor in Wolfsburg and made just a few stops along the way.

From time to time I could see tall, energy-producing propeller windmills in the distance. Germany produces a good deal of renewable energy. I arrived in Frankfurt in the early evening. My hotel was within walking distance of the train station. The area around the station was a little seedy, but I wasn't going to be in Frankfurt for long.

I checked into the hotel and went for a walk and after a while I came across the European Central Bank headquarters marked by a large sculpture of the euro symbol in front. Eventually I reached a pedestrian mall lined with fine stores. I took my time window shopping and walking; making up for my seclusion in the Green Zone. At the end of the mall I came to a street fair that stretched for blocks. I took in the sights, looked at souvenirs, had a beer and a bratwurst and then took a taxi back to the hotel. It was 10 or 11 p.m. by the time I reached the hotel and the district's seediness was in flower. But I had no time for play, I had to go to the base in the morning.

Wiesbaden is about an hour away from Frankfurt by train. There were two American businessmen riding in the same car with me and I struck up a conversation. They were surprised to hear that I was in Iraq; they thought that with the war over we had withdrawn all of our troops. I told them what was really going on. I supposed that when a war goes on for as long as this one has it simply fades in popular consciousness and becomes merely background noise.

The Wiesbaden airfield was the home of Herman Göring's first Luftwaffe base. The base at Wiesbaden was one of the first seized by the United States in Germany during the Second World War; it will probably be one of the last given up. There had been an American base in Frankfurt, but it had closed. I took a taxi to the base's entrance. I approached the German guard, who seeing me without a uniform, thought I was merely a tourist he needed to shoo away. I showed him my LoA and he called for American back-up. As is the case at all U.S. embassies overseas, the local nationals are the first line of defense.

An American soldier came by shortly. He looked at the LoA and I explained to him that I had come from Iraq because CAAC cards were no longer being issued in theater. He nodded and told me how to get to the base ID office, a short walk away.

I arrived at the base ID office. Unlike the bases in Iraq, the construction was similar to U.S. bases that I had visited before. Louisiana, Panama, Great Lakes and now Germany—they all had the same feel. Iraq was very different. Iraq was an occupation and any construction was ad hoc.

I wasn't the first defense contractor to come to Wiesbaden for credentials. The officer looked at my

LoA, took my biometric data, had me fill out a few forms, and then I went to the waiting room to await processing.

The officer apologized that since I was not posted to Germany that I would not have access to the base PX or post office, but reassured me that the stores in Frankfurt and Wiesbaden would have everything that I couldn't get in Iraq. Within an hour or so, I was back with the German guard asking him the best way to get back to town. He recommended a bus and motioned to a bus stop a hundred yards or so from the gate. In a few minutes a bus came by, taking me and the newly-issued CAAC card in my pocket back to the train station.

By early evening I was back in Berlin and called Liz. I had met Liz at the Helmut Newton champagne bar in Mitte. She heard me struggling with German and stepped in to translate. She said that she was from Chicago; we had gone to the same university. In addition to German, which she spoke fluently, she spoke Arabic. She was studying for an advanced degree and had lived in Berlin for a year or so. She suggested that we meet at Café Einstein, a speakeasy-type Weimar themed bar in the Tiergarten district, It sounded good to me. Later, though, she sent me an SMS that said we should meet at the Reingold Cocktail Bar in Mitte instead.

It was a place I never would have found myself. I arrived first; she came in wearing a light, long coat and boots. There was just a hint of autumn in the air, it was cool in Berlin at night. She told me that she had finished her new article and that some of her pieces were posted on the Internet. She was thinking about going back to Chicago to finish her degree. She just needed one or two courses; she was close enough so not to finish would be a waste. Nevertheless, she would be sorry to leave Berlin. She had a good life in the city, and while her job didn't pay the best at least her articles were published regularly in an English magazine that was eagerly read locally.

She wondered if she could get a job with a newspaper in Chicago; I told her of the demise of the City News Bureau and my one visit to their office many years ago. Then she said that maybe she would return to Palestine; she had taught English in Ramallah and her Arabic was pretty good. I tested her with a few phrases and she responded immediately. Her Arabic was far, far better than mine. I told her that speaking Arabic could open doors and suggested she might look for a position with a network or as a stringer. Newspapers and networks were cutting costs and now relied on independent correspondents.

We left the speakeasy later and walked to an Indonesian restaurant serving *rijkstaffel*. I told her that I might be coming back to Berlin during my periodic leave from Baghdad. She said for 500 euro per month I wouldn't have too much difficulty finding an apartment. If she were still in Berlin she would help me find an apartment in Berlin.

She told me that she would probably be back in Chicago in a month or two. I told her that I hoped I would see her again. It is important to have plans for the future, especially when you are going to a war zone. So we made plans, for I was going back to war.

Back in Baghdad

September 14

BACK IN BAGHDAD. Berlin was great. The only bad thing about the city was the arrival at the unprepared Shönefeld airport and the fact that stores were closed on Sunday.

Because I had been up all night, I wasn't that observant on the ride coming in. I did notice that Duncan, the Scotsman in charge of the operation to bring me to the Green Zone, made me wear body armor. I hadn't worn body army in the car before, it was quite heavy and uncomfortable. He told me that things had been quiet in Baghdad, but if so, why the body armor?

We came straight to the Sabre compound and I ran into Ahmed. I was surprised to see him since he is supposed to be bedridden in Amman. He is remarkably healthy after his operation. I picked up the key to my room—they had given me the same room—and went to sleep. I didn't even put my Iraqi SIM card in the phone because I needed to sleep before dealing with office matters.

I enjoyed the trip to Berlin but spent too much money. Air Berlin services the city. So does easyJet. Maybe next time I'll go to Spain or Ireland. I don't know if I'll be back before Liz leaves.

September 15

I'm still recovering from the Berlin trip. I don't feel well. I was up all night. I have stomach pains. Major problem—my phone charger didn't arrive. I might have left it in Berlin. When the battery winds down, I won't have a phone.

Florian has started up his old antics again.

September 16

Things are very quiet in Baghdad. The sirens have not gone off once since my arrival on Tuesday. Perhaps everything really is calm, the war is over. I can only think that Al Qaeda and ISI (Islamic State of Iraq) are planning something special for us, something very big.

There was an attack on Monday on a joint patrol in Fallujah. Seven people were killed. It was a joint patrol just like all the other joint patrols. The target was a former colonel in the old Iraqi army. Civilians were killed in the process. When that happens it is very, very bad.

Yesterday a U.S. soldier was killed while defusing a roadside bomb 40 miles or so north of Baghdad. I don't care what anybody says, the country is still at war. Maybe that's why they had me wear body armor in the car.

At dinner I met a black American named Scotty, he's from New Orleans and Atlanta. He is a contractor working at FOB Shield, about 500 meters from Sadr City. He told me that there are 43 Iraqi Army checkpoints you have to go through before you reach the base. I'm not sure if he means there are precisely 43 because he has counted them or not. In Arabic, saying "over 40" is a way to say "many."

I've made some progress on the APO and I hope to get it tomorrow. Unfortunately, everything here is so difficult.

September 17

I found out that in order to get APO access Sabre needs a mail officer. Since they don't have one, I signed up for the qualifying postal training class at FOB Union III. If I pass the course I should be able to start receiving APO mail.

I found my phone charger today. It had somehow hidden itself inside a suitcase.

A Man with Breasts

I SPENT THE DAY writing an emergency memorandum on sex change rules in Iraq. The country is going to hell and the Americans are wondering what Iraqi rules apply to a man with breasts.

For most lawyers, determining the law is usually a matter of reviewing statutes or case law in an effort to apply them to a particular set of facts. Sometimes the facts can be distinguished from a particular case; sometimes a statute clearly doesn't apply. A lawyer who can make a good faith argument that the law needs to be changed is obligated to do so, but this obligation is tempered by a judge's duty to follow settled law.

Difficult or unusual issues always seem to come up on the last day of the week or when offices in other countries are closed. The client wanted an immediate decision. Urgently.

A defense contractor was about to board a plane for Iraq. Either his employer was a diversity-promoting, open-minded paragon of non-discrimination or blind. Or maybe somehow due diligence failed, or the background investigation and security clearance never went beyond the two possible answers to the question asking for gender identification. Hours before the flight was to take off, someone realized that perhaps the Iraqis would not be as liberal as Americans when it comes to the question of a man with breasts.

The question put to me was really, "can we still send him?" but of course it was not phrased that way. So I had to research Iraqi law in order to determine what would be the likely legal position of the Iraqi government. But there was a twist: the contractor had not reached the end of the new gender identity road. So a medical examination would reveal that the contractor with breasts was still biologically a man.

Answering a question such as this should not be undertaken on a Friday afternoon in the Green Zone. There are cultural conventions, military regulations—in short, a regulatory swamp that has to be navigated. U.S. military prisons must accommodate prisoners seeking gender reassignment. The condition is treated like any other medical condition. In Iraq, the matter was not so clear.

In Iraq, religious issues are always front and center. Shi'a and Sunni might well have different views. There were practical issues as well. While Michael Jackson had romped around shopping malls in Bahrain while wearing an abaya without incurring the attention of the police, other men who had donned the traditional black robe worn by Gulf women had been arrested and charged with disorderly conduct. Since defense contractors no longer had immunity from arrest, this was a real possibility.

The clock was ticking.

I was surprised at what I found. Shocked, really. Which country has paid for more sex change operations than any other? Which political leader could be seen as the most compassionate in this regard? In the United States, I'm guessing that the only way to get the government to pay for sex-reassignment surgery is to find a way into a federal prison. A military one, preferably, since they have recent institutional experience.

Or you could go to Iran.

Though Iran, like most Muslim countries, has outlawed homosexuality, Iranian Shi'a thinkers such as Ayatollah Khomeini have allowed transsexuals to change their gender so that they can enter heterosexual relationships. This position has been confirmed by the current Supreme Leader of Iran, Ayatollah Ali Khamenei, and is also supported by many other Iranian clerics. The state will pay a portion of the cost for a sex-change operation. Despite support for transsexuals from Iranian religious leaders, Iranian society itself is less accepting of them. Iraq does not pay for gender reassignment surgery.

In Iraq, individual cases are reviewed on a case by case basis by the Ministry of the Interior and appointed religious scholars. Transgender candidates are not arrested. There is no general shari'a rule which applies to individuals who seek gender reassignment and have not completed the process.

I was surprised to find that the Ministry of Health in 2002 promulgated a formal Instruction on the subject. Though the Instruction on its face only applies to Iraqi nationals, it is expressive of local attitudes. An individual seeking gender reassignment will be subject to a medical and psychological review. If gender reassignment is permitted, a legal official will be appointed to advise on the legal consequences. This refers to the different status of men and women under the Islamic shari'a, especially in matters of divorce and inheritance.

A person who has completed gender reassignment surgery will have his identity documents amended to reflect the new status and thereafter can expect to be treated as female under the law.

Bringing a pre-op transgendered individual to Iraq was not a good idea: there were simply two many possibilities for mischief. Once the operation was completed Iraq was, at least legally, tolerant of these individuals.

After finding these references I was able to meet the deadline and put together a short legal opinion to send to the client, who then gave the bad news to the contractor.

In a war zone anything can happen. All in all, it was not a bad day's work for a Friday in the Green Zone.

September 18

The day of my postal class at FOB Union III. I arrived around 11:45 for a class at 1 p.m. The class was held in the former Ba'ath Party headquarters on the base. The Nepalese driver left me off at a roundabout in front of the base. He has been in Iraq for five years. He asks me if I have any influence with the military. Since I am an American, I must have connections. Here success depends on taking advantage of your connections. He is worried because his CAAC card is expiring and since the cards can no longer be issued in Iraq, he will lose his job.

I walked towards the back of the building, passing by all sorts of soldiers in uniform, many of them carrying automatic weapons. I passed the DFAC and more people came out, headed into the palace. At the end of the palace there was some kind of Iraqi-run tiki hut outdoor bar but it was closed. But at the end of the building it was impossible to reach the other side. I asked a civilian how I could get to the other side. He was outside the back of the palace taking a smoking break. Smoking is prohibited inside. We have saved Saddam's palaces from the evil of tobacco. The directions he gave me were incoherent.

I entered the palace and soon became trapped in a maze. I passed through the MWR (Morale, Welfare, Recreation) area. There was a movie theater.

A huge television screen in front of couches. An Internet café. A line of LCD screens in front of easy chairs—I found out later that these were for soldiers waiting to play video games. There was a library with couches in it also. A lot of the couches were filled with soldiers trying to sleep. One was riveted on whatever was on his laptop's screen, but the most common activity was sleeping. Down in front of the movie theater's screen a female soldier snuggled with a male soldier in the front row. Later, she stood up, slung an M-16 across her back and walked away.

I saw other soldiers at Internet terminals which had been set up for their use. Some simply played video games while others watched videos, checked Facebook or spoke to friends or family in the United States. While connected, they could have been anywhere—even around the corner. But they weren't. The Iraq war is the world's first connected war. Previously, when soldiers went off to war they connected with those back home by letter and the odd telephone call. Now they can go on patrol in the morning in Iraq and still connect with friends and family who wake up seven hours later. The Internet connection creates the illusion that the soldiers are closely connected with those back home—maybe just as connected as they were before they deployed. After all, you don't see your friends every day. But the connection is an illusion, for as long as they are in Iraq there can be no physical connection. When they are on the Internet, they are home. Then the next day, they drive through Sadr City in the Red Zone where their lives are at extreme risk. You're home and you're not. How this affects soldiers in the long term is an open question.

While the media so often focused on the few American deserters, to me what was more interesting were the soldiers who signed up for additional tours. For whatever reason, here more than anywhere else they felt alive, useful; the connection of being a part of a team and accomplishing a mission they saw as critical was important to them. The same was true for the contractors.

When I reached as far as I could go, a team of civilians took pity on this obviously lost fellow-traveler and escorted me to the other side of the building. As it turns out, for the class I had to return to the MWR area and wait. Despite all my walking around the palace, I was still about a half hour early.

Eventually Lt. Brigitte Williams, US Navy, came in and taught the class. She explained what to do and what not to do. Prohibited items are basically anything mentioned in General Order No. 1.

The primary concern of the class, overriding all others, was to teach us what to do with mail addressed to the dead. This was a very, very big issue. We were not supposed to open such mail or write on it. It had to specially be put aside. While other mail could be forwarded, mail addressed to the dead was different.

At the end of the class, Lt. Williams helped us fill out our paperwork and we were given a test. I had trouble remembering all of the form numbers we had discussed in class but I passed. We were all told to return the next day with our Letters of Authorization to get our mail clerk ID cards.

I called Ops and they said they would send someone to pick me up. As I approached the entrance to the camp I heard a mortar explode. I later learned it was an 81 mm shell. One or two soldiers started running towards the direction of fire, but then they stopped. I went into the PX for a while and then walked out of the camp. When I walked out, the sirens went off and the Ugandan soldiers near the entrance hurried into a duck and cover. I ran to join them. They crouched down and put on their helmets. There were seven Ugandan soldiers and me. I was standing, there wasn't enough room for me to get down. They weren't making any room for me either. The "all clear" finally came and I left the shelter and crossed the road. A few minutes later the Nepalese driver turned up to collect me. He asked me if I had any news about his CAAC card.

September 19

Sunday. At 0845 I heard some kind of detonation. There was another at 0930, 1020 and 1245. The insurgency is making up for its days of silence. There were so many alarms I thought it might not be possible to return to FOB Union III to deliver my paperwork. In the end it turned out not to be a problem. I arrived and this time easily made my way to the mail unit. Lt. Brigitte gave me my Unit Mail Clerk card. I am now officially a Unit Mail Clerk in addition to all of my other duties.

Envelopes sent via military mail from Iraq will bear a cancellation which reads "US FORCES IRAQ" so at least there is no doubt where the mail will be coming from. If this law gig doesn't work out, perhaps I can get a job with the post office back home.

The Sabre compound had a small bar that was open in the evenings. Not anyone could just enter the premises; you had to be a resident or a guest. It was one of the few places in the Green Zone where you could get a drink. General Order No. 1 did not apply.

One evening, I found myself at the bar. I had just gotten back from Berlin and had only a 50 euro note, which was worth about $75. Only U.S. currency was accepted at the bar, or for that matter, anywhere else in the Green Zone. I never saw Iraqi dinars. There were foreign exchange shops and the ATM's only dispensed dollars.

I tried to pay with the Euros, but no one wanted them. An Irishman offered to buy them from me—for two U.S. twenty dollar bills. I told him that no one would take euros in the Green Zone. He was insistent, I agreed. After he placed the bills in my hand he loudly announced what a fool I was because he had just doubled his money in the transaction, yada yada. About an hour later I heard him trying to exchange the 50 euro note. No one wanted it. It was useless until he got back to Ireland. Who got the better deal?

September 20

Yesterday was a day of coordinated attacks. The worst was in Fallujah where 26 people died in a car bomb explosion. There were three serious car bombings throughout the country on the 19th. This morning, the first alarm came came before 4:00 a.m., and by 9:00 there had been a total of three separate alarms. The hazy weather gives the insurgency cover and they take advantage of it. Otherwise the helicopters would follow and it would be too dangerous. Bad weather is the time to attack targets.

There is a new kidnapping threat but I am not really worried. Anyone who would kidnap me for ransom should be aware that there is no pot of gold at the end of the kidnap rainbow.

Florian sent over a contract from Dubai and asked me to take a look at it. The governing law would be Saudi. I read through the contract but I had difficulty understanding what the commercial purpose of the agreement was, if there was even any commercial activity. One of the problems with being a business lawyer is that you often have to say "no." For this reason many managers will move heaven and earth so that they can avoid involving their company's legal department, because they know their lawyers will push back.

September 21

There were two alarms today. Compared to last week, things are much worse, though Iraq is supposedly now at peace. I spent much of the day working on a litigation report for a case involving the Coalition Provisional Authority. Florian called at 10 p.m. and had me on the phone for an hour. This is abusive. I went back to the room and watched a movie. I wrote a few comments about Baghdad on Facebook but then I realized I was attention-whoring so I deleted my post. Trying to be a part of a virtual community or keep virtual friends provides only the illusion of a real connection.

It is not really possible to stay in touch with anyone in the United States, despite e-mail and despite the Internet. Because of the time difference, the widening gap between shared experiences and the loss of common frames of reference, friends grow apart. You don't realize this at first because initially it seems as though nothing has changed. You see your friends' posts, they see yours. But inexorably you drift away.

September 22

There were two sirens so far today. The first came at 13:35 with two detonations, one after another. Instead of a siren, an amplified voice on the loudspeakers warned, "Incoming, Incoming." This is the first time there has been a voice warning. In the afternoon there were two more attacks for a total of four so far today. The press doesn't pick up on these at all. These attacks are not reported.

The mortar rounds were a lot closer today. Some in the compound were afraid.

A French company wants to set up in Iraq. Immediately. I told that it normally takes about six months to obtain all the necessary permissions. Or, you can buy a shelf company. They asked me to explain what a shelf company was so I told them. While they were going back and forth talking to Paris about the advisability of buying a shelf company, another client came in and offered to buy the only existing shelf company in our Iraqi inventory. Unfortunately, Ahmed overlooked sharing this news with me. So now the French want to fly in and sign and there is no more shelf company to sell them.

I'm constantly caught between Florian and our Iraqi clients. It's pretty pathetic that the stress from the job is worse than the stress from the mortars. Baghdad isn't the problem, the firm is.

September 23

The mortar attacks continue. I thought that I would have an easy day but there was a conference call at 7 p.m. There is never a break, it's always, "we need this immediately." People would like to forget that we are in a war zone. This is easy to do because officially it's not a war zone anymore.

September 24

It is somewhat amusing to me that I am more worried about Florian's complaints than I am about the shelling. Tonight there were three mortar attacks. The first was very close at 20:49, the second came at 21:49 and the third at 22:54. Each one was about an hour apart. The first one was the loudest.

October

October 2

FOR THE PAST week I have been ill. Today was the first day I was able to return to work. Last Monday I woke up at 04:00, having gone to bed at 17:00 the previous day. I woke up vomiting badly. I spent Monday in bed; on Tuesday it was worse. On Wednesday Ops checked up on me after no one had seen me come out of my room for two days. They took me to the military clinic at FOB Prosperity. There, the doctors put me on an IV and gave me a lidocaine cocktail to drink. It was the first time I'd seen a doctor treating patients while wearing a .45 pistol. All the medical personnel were armed.

I think everyone thought I was faking until they got my lab work back. "My friend, I don't really know what you have, but you are SICK," the doctor told me. He has to deal with goldbricking soldiers who feign illness to get out of duty. Perhaps he thought that I was one of these.

A combat medic treated me, mostly, but when the shift changed he was replaced by an African American woman who attended to me while an M-

16 hung a strap on her shoulder. She seemed suspicious of me, for some reason. Perhaps she thought I was taking the place of a real soldier. I couldn't blame her.

They kept me for the whole afternoon and wouldn't let me go until I had drained a second IV bag.

One does not normally associate firearms with physicians, surgeons and nurses in the United States. When was the last time you saw a nurse packing an M-16? But we're not in the U.S. anymore.

We're in Iraq.

October 3

Ops has announced that there is now a serious risk of kidnapping. So I guess no more walks to the Fedex office in the morning. Am I worried about this new warning? Not really. Putting it all together, what it means is that there is no way at all this place will normalize in the next year. It's simply impossible. Florian disagrees. He says that things will normalize in a year.

He continues to pick at the legal opinions. Why write that the ship "sailed" if the ship had diesel engines? Hours of agony. Three hours today on bullshit. The cough I had last week returned so, so there's another medical condition to deal with. It's probably stress-related. Florian's micromanagement is intolerable and causes me a good deal of stress.

Here in the compound it's like kindergarten: if one child gets sick, they all get sick. That's why the there are hand sanitizers outside the entrance to the cafeteria.

There's a reception tomorrow at the German Embassy in celebration of Reunification Day. Attending embassy receptions is a good opportunity to network and keep a finger on the pulse of a country.

The United States has issued a travel advisory for Western Europe; but so what? Europe is nothing compared to almost daily shelling.

October 4

I went into the Red Zone for the first time today, wearing a bulletproof vest. The destination was the German Embassy and the event, German Reunification Day. We are a German firm so we have been invited. The event began at three in the afternoon.

On the way to the Red Zone traffic lights were working and we stopped for them.

At the German Embassy, ambassadors from other countries and invited guests broke off into small groups. Security personnel who guarded their country's representative filtered into and out of the reception. There was a group of heavily armed Chinese guards dressed in black. They looked like ninjas.

The Ambassador's speech was lengthy and non-controversial; a prayer for peace. In Iraq Ambassador's are targets and only a brave man will accept the assignment. I was reminded of all the similar embassy parties in Riyadh, except that no one drank desperately. I didn't drink at all. Mixing alcohol, body armor and the insurgency is a bad recipe.

October 5

My trip to the Red Zone yesterday confirmed that I will never be free to walk in the streets here. I will always be under some kind of protective restrictions. Still, some risk regular travel throughout the country. I met a German businessman who ignored the kidnapping threats and had driven, by himself, to Erbil. He was stopped by militiamen and taken to a small town, where a village elder, after determining he was not American, asked for his help in rebuilding his village, which had been badly damaged by the war. Some, at least, were mobile in Iraq.

But not all.

The surprise was seeing that in the evening the traffic lights were working. On the way to the German Embassy we passed the ruins of the Ar-Rahman mosque, the largest mosque in the world. Saddam didn't finish it before the war started, but even the ruins are spectacular. The ruins lie in the middle of an enormous plain. Dozens of abandoned cranes stand still connected to the unfinished construction works. Saddam tried to build the largest mosque in the world with room for 100,000 at prayer. Numerous cranes surround the abandoned structure. The building was a reminder of an Iraq that is no more.

The afternoon was crazy with work. Florian harassing as usual. A lawyer must always remember that the most insignificant matter may blow up spectacularly at any time, and it is always the most insignificant matter that contains the possibility of the greatest danger.

★★★

The last case I worked on in Iraq involved a group of investors who was happy to sell their shares in a company, cash the checks, and then pretend as if the transaction never occurred. I have never been able to understand why people do this. When you defraud people you know, you will be caught. There will be consequences. You are already working in a system with rules. You may profit momentarily, but the day will come when your new Mercedes is taken from your driveway and loaded onto a flat bad truck and hauled away. It is one thing to be smart in business, to take advantage of a perceived opportunity. Doing something stupid, like stealing property that doesn't belong to you, is never the smart thing to do. The problem is that stupid people believe they are clever.

Fakry Ibrahim Shanshal and his brothers sold their shares of Al-Seqir Express Cargo to a firm client. Though they received value for their shares, they refused to register their shares in the name of the new shareholders. They then fired the Al-Seqir's director and had the signatories changed on the company's bank accounts. My client found out when he tried to use his ATM. These matters eventually get resolved, but the law is a slow-moving machine. The client, on the other hand, was desperate.

The client called me, frantic, on a Friday afternoon. His ATM card wasn't working. He contacted the bank and was told that his signature was no longer on the firm's accounts. Sorry, they told him, you need to talk to a lawyer. He could reach no one in Dubai, where the company had its headquarters. So he called me.

He wanted only one thing from me—a demand letter directed to the Shanshals putting them on notice that they had committed fraud. He was sure that this would bring them to their senses. I had a general sense of the transaction since we had handled the joint venture agreement. Fraud was not supposed to be a part of the deal.

I tried to reach Florian, but couldn't. He had been traveling—to Vancouver and then to South America—but was now back in Germany. Unfortunately he was asleep. He liked to take a siesta during the day. For a critical four-hour period during which the client became increasingly frantic, Florian was nowhere to be found.

At lunchtime Hassan Ferris called asking me to reformat the text of a demand letter he wanted to send to Dubai. He wanted to send the letter out by close of business in Dubai, one hour ahead of Baghdad. His company's accounts had been frozen by a creditor despite the fact that an arbitration was pending. He was desperate. Because Florian wanted everything coordinated, I sent Florian an e-mail apprising him of the situation and telling him that if he wanted to get involved that I would have to hear from him by 1500 because the client wanted the letter sent before 1600 Baghdad time.

I worked with Hassan on the demand letter. We went through three drafts before he was finally satisfied. The letter was firm, but not hysterical, and warned:

> "any action you take with respect to Al-Seqir without the consent of the majority shareholder is improper. Consequently, your use of the Al-Seqir letterhead without the consent of the majority shareholder is improper, your reference to yourselves in the letter as the "shareholders" in Al-Seqir is false and any action you take as the pur-

> ported "shareholders" in Al-Seqir is also
> false and tantamount to fraud."

I waited. Every ten minutes or so Hassan called to ask if I had heard from Florian yet, and urging me to sign and send the letter anyway. By 1515 I had received no reply from Florian. Sending a fax would take more than just a few minutes. I put the letter on a USB stick and walked it over to Operations, printed it and faxed it to the Shanshals.

There was no immediate response.

Two hours later, Florian called me frantically, questioning my decision to send the demand letter, moaning that there were other ways to handle the matter, that I should have contacted him, why oh why did I send the letter?

He was belittling as usual. He then stated that he had spoken with his partner Stephan and neither of them could believe that I had signed such a letter. He attempted to edit the letter but Hassan did not like his proposed changes anyway. All of this was academic: the counterparty had already received the demand to release the funds.

I told Florian that he had been asleep and unreachable, the client's need was urgent and I made a decision that it was appropriate to help the client. After all, helping clients is our business. This was a crisis. Someone had to make a decision. There was no one else who could make it, so I did.

October 5 193

Florian told me to pack up and leave the Green Zone.

$\star \atop \star \; \star$

I do not regret making the decision and if presented with the same facts today I would take the exact same action. Florian's fears were imaginary. However the matter would shake out, it would not be resolved on a Friday afternoon and it was unlikely a demand letter would resolve anything. Still, the client knew his partners and knew how to negotiate with them. While a lawyer should not blindly obey a client's request, this request was reasonable. Florian's unhappiness with the transaction could only mean that something else was going on and that there was more to the story that neither he, the client nor the Shanshals were telling me.

The next day Brad Thompson from Operations came into the office and handed me a letter advising me that I would have to leave the compound. But by then I had already told everyone I was leaving.

I'm not sure how I feel. I suppose I should feel bad, but I'm happy that I will no longer have to deal with Florian. I don't know what I'll do. I really don't. Ahmed continues to be AWOL and I am more or less running the Iraqi operation alone. The Erbil office, after all, is illusory. I'm sure they'll muddle through without me, one way or another. I don't believe Florian will change his mind. I guess we will see what happens next. I thought that if I worked hard and put up with the bullshit things would work out. But they didn't.

I need some time to figure out what is the next course of action.

October 6

The sirens sounded at 05:00 but I didn't hear them. I was up all night. I couldn't sleep. My life is going to change and I don't know what direction it's going to take. It wasn't that long ago—only last June—that I bought this diary.

I had breakfast at 07:30 and then went up to the office and started downloading my files from the office laptop and backing up the hard drive. I finished shortly after 09:00, but by then Munich had already locked me out of Outlook, preventing me from backing-up e-mail addresses. It didn't matter, given the instability of electricity in the Green Zone, I already had back-ups I then went to Ops. Tony was there and invited me in for a coffee. I told him what had happened. I got a ride to the APO and found out that I can mail a footlocker without any problem. Finally the APO access has paid off.

I went to FOB Union and bought three footlockers, packing materials and then returned to the Sabre compound. Brad Taylor came by and handed me my termination letter. I sent a note to Florian asking to reconsider his decision. He responded to my response by not responding.

Five hours later he sent me an e-mail asking me to finish several assignments. I told him that he had to be kidding. He offered to pay and said he would pay if I worked the weekend in Dubai and brought the people in the office there up to speed. I called Liam Mooney, the recruiter who had referred me to Florian; he was flabbergasted.

I finished packing around 3 p.m. but by then it was too late to take the footlockers back to the APO. Florian sent an e-mail insisting that I leave Iraq immediately. Since he can shut me out of Sabre I really don't have a choice.

I am really quite tired but still running on adrenalin and unable to sleep. Perhaps I will sleep better tonight.

How strange is life. One day and everything turns around.

October 7

Got up in the morning and went to the APO at FOB Union. I had forgotten my Letter of Authorization and so had to come back to get it. The footlocker weighed 55 pounds and but it only cost $34 to ship it to Atlanta. Two boxes of books cost only an additional $20. It would have cost $300 or more to take all of this with me as excess baggage if they would even have let me do so—the memory of the Ugandan soldiers repacking at the airport was still fresh. Schlepping all of these boxes through airports would be a logistical nightmare. I wouldn't be traveling light.

Though Florian threw me out unexpectedly, he has no intention of offering me a severance package. Instead, he wants me to finish various assignments for which he'll pay me the rest of my October salary, if my work is up to par, in his sole judgment. Fool me once…I call my travel agent in Miami and tell him to buy a ticket for me from Dubai back to Miami. I'll pick up my truck and take things from there.

Florian asked me to meet with Jochen Murach in Dubai to work on a few pending matters and to brief him on the status of the Baghdad office. When I contacted Jochen, he told me that he was not available and had other plans for the weekend. Florian had failed to check with Jochen before setting up the meeting. I told Jochen to enjoy his weekend. Now there's really no reason for me to go to Dubai at all. I don't have an exit visa to leave Iraq yet, so I am in no particular rush. I don't want to go on a junket to Dubai because now I really have to be careful with money—I am unemployed.

I never visited the office in the Red Zone. To do so was expensive, I would have needed a security detail and Florian never wanted to pay for that.

Ahmed said that if I went with him I would probably be murdered, so it was best that I didn't go. I saw no reason to argue with him. In hindsight, it is unlikely that there was ever an office in the Red Zone.

I am sure that the address was a real building, and if you visited it you could probably even go up the stairs, open the door and sit down. Maybe it was Ahmed's other office. Maybe it was a friendly lawyer who let us use his address. I don't really know. The Red Zone office was like our Erbil office: aspirational; cosmetic: it looks good on paper until you try to visit. If this were really one company there should have been a team in the Red Zone working. But there was no team; that was aspirational too.

No one from the other Baghdad office ever stopped by to meet me. For an Iraqi citizen, getting through the checkpoints was onerous, but not impossible, especially one with legitimate business in the Green Zone. But no one ever came.

Then there were Ahmed's strange absences. He was in the office at most once per week, and then only in the evenings. When I came upstairs after dinner and found the door unlocked I was always surprised. When there was a meeting or a need for him to come during the day there was always an excuse. A bombing. The death of a friend. A sudden illness. He needed to go to Jordan, the only easy getaway for Iraqis where life was normal.

When he did contribute his work was most worthwhile. But he was never there.

All of a sudden I realized that I knew why Ahmed was always out of the office and appeared only at nights. He had another job. Sometimes what is right before your eyes isn't obvious. The simplest explanations usually, but not always, are the right ones. He rarely appeared during the day because he couldn't get away. He appeared from time to time at night because he was no longer on duty somewhere else. He was in the Green Zone when there was somewhere else he didn't have to be.

The answer was in right in front of me, but I didn't see it. Obviously Ahmed had another job. That is why he could never show up during the day. It was the simplest explanation. Perhaps Amir Kordvani figured what he was up to and for this reason was let go. The nonsense about "insulting" Ahmed could only be that: pure nonsense. Ahmed may have had to concoct a story simply to protect his other job. I was merely an incredulous American. Since I couldn't go to the Red Zone, he could make up whatever stories he wanted and I had no choice to but to believe them.

The firm did have real offices in Cairo and Dubai where real work was done. I had, after all, visited them. There was the office in Berlin, with another company's name on the door. All the pieces of the puzzle started falling into place. The firm punched above its weight, to be sure, but much of it was virtual; in reality was quite different from its paper profile.

None of this mattered now. If Florian's clients were happy, good for them. If Ahmed was double-dipping, that was his problem, not mine. In a few hours I would be in Manama.

In Dubai I'll consider the options for my future. I thought it was planned out for a while, but that turned out not to be the case. Now we'll see what's really going to happen.

October 8

A Sabre Security soldier named Duncan is in charge of my security detail. We were going to leave a little early because Ops had other commitments for the afternoon. Florian had asked Ahmed Al-Marid to arrange for unprotected transportation to the airport. Florian's idea was that Ahmed would just take me to the airport himself, with no security at all. I'm not sure if this was simply additional harassment or if there was some other motive. I couldn't even say goodbye to Ahmed. I hadn't seen him in a while. He was unreachable and supposedly wasn't even in the country, which is typical Florian—issuing orders to imaginary armies. I told Florian that I had already made arrangements through Sabre. After all, he was the one who insisted that I leave immediately.

After I finished packing, I was invited to a barbecue on the compound. A fire was built and those of us who were living at Sabre sat around it in a circle. The conversation mostly focused on the current situation in Iraq and where in Europe you could buy one of the new unlocked iPhones. It might have been a barbecue anywhere in the U.S. or the U.K. But it wasn't. The more they tried to make it like home the further away it was. But the difference is that I was going home.

I left the next morning. Because it was Friday, there was almost no traffic. The security detail was more relaxed this time. It has been two or three days since the last mortar attack. I was told to wear the black body armor anyway. The back plate dug into my back a little and I thought of all the journalists wearing this uncomfortable gear as they reported from the streets of Baghdad. Did the need to get out of the armor hurry their reporting?

The road to the airport was almost empty. There was nothing remarkable and we arrived in less than half an hour. I said goodbye to the detail and made my own way through the multiple security checkpoints to the Gulf Air check-in counter for the flight to Manama. Security was the same as before.

We didn't use the jetway and boarded a bus to

take us to the Airbus which was parked far from the terminal on a tarmac. The airplane was far enough away so that if the terminal building came under fire, it would be safe unless it had been specifically targeted. The flight was full. At least Florian had purchased a business class ticket. I figured that he had done so begrudgingly only because he wanted me out of Sabre right away and there were no seats left in economy class. As I walked up the stairs to the cabin I turned around on the landing to look at Baghdad for one last time. After boarding we sat on the ramp for fifteen minutes or so with doors still open in case we needed to evacuate. Finally the truck-mounted staircase pulled away, a pilot closed the cockpit door, the doors were closed and engines started.

At 12:30 we took off. The plane made several turns leaving the airport. The flight to Bahrain would take two hours. Iraq was over.

Bahrain—Dubai

BAHRAIN WAS NORMAL in a world that had not been normal for a long time. There were no soldiers on patrol, no Mad Max pieced together trucks or Humvees with booms wrapped with wires hanging for three meters in front of the engines, no electronic countermeasures to cause your mobile phone to fail. The concourse was the same as I had seen it on my previous trips from Riyadh. The normalcy and abundance were unsettling. Saudis dressed in white or black strolled down the concourse; men from the Subcontinent lined up for their flights home. The war was far away.

There have been a few cosmetic improvements to the airport in Bahrain but nothing significant. I still had some Bahraini dinars from the last time I visited the country while I was living in Saudi Arabia. Seen with Saudi eyes Bahrain is an extraordinarily free country, but I no longer have Saudi eyes.

No one acted as if there was a war. A thousand miles away a fuel carrier had to be armored and sirens called to shelter in concrete bunkers on a football pitch. Here rocket attacks are unheard of. Bahrain defines itself in terms of its differences from its neighbors. Coming from war, these differences were extreme.

No one cared where I had been, no one congratulated me on having survived.

A few hours later I was checked in for my flight to Dubai, farther away still from the war. From Dubai there there were no flights back to Iraq. There was no immediate way to get back. It was odd that I was already wondering how I might go back.

The flight to Dubai was delayed. Because of the delay I was given a first class seat which was luxurious. All I could think of was how great it would be to have that seat while crossing the Atlantic back to Atlanta.

By 19:00 I was in Dubai. The airport was deserted: Dubai's economy had tanked and the country had fallen fast and hard. The taxi to the Metropolitan Hotel on Sheikh Zayed Road took just twenty minutes. There was almost no traffic.

The war was one further step removed and no one cared about it at all. Apartments were empty on Sheikh Zayed road not because people had tired of the sirens and shelling or mortar fire or roadside bombs but because collateralized debt obligations had blown up in Iceland taking down one economy after another. In Dubai construction employees drove themselves to the airport and abandoning their cars, credit card debt and dreams of early retirement. The vehicles had to be removed, eight at a time, on trucks. The only way to tell which cars were abandoned was by the accumulation of dust. Airport workers would write a date in the dust and if it was still there a week later the car would be towed away.

October 9 Dubai

I woke up late after sleeping in. There were several e-mails from Jochen asking me to meet him at 10:00 in the office. After days of protests complaining that he had other unalterable commitments, all of a sudden he is available. Obviously, Florian had finally reached him and ordered him to cancel his weekend plans. I sent a note to Florian telling him that I had read his note proposing that I work for a few days in Dubai and that it was unacceptable. He has made it clear that he is not paying any severance; I have made it clear that I am ignoring him. I am letting him stew. Because I am already in Dubai there is nothing he can do. He has no leverage. Tomorrow I will return to Atlanta. At this point I honestly don't think there can be any change.

October 10

I got up early and left the hotel for the Dubai International Airport before dawn. Life went on normally in the airport. I checked in to my British Airways flight. A few hours later I was on my way to London; and after a brief stopover, I continued on to Atlanta.

When I reached Atlanta there was a group of soldiers assembling near baggage claim. Their uniforms were as fresh as their backpacks and other gear. Their boots had not walked the dust of the Middle East. I walked past them; I wanted to wish them good luck. But I could not do so. Their novice commander would have ordered them to ignore me. I wanted to tell them to be careful.

Instead I walked out into the light and the taxi stand. I gave an address to the dispatcher and waited for a cab.

I have left the house of war.

Miami

IN SOME WAYS, I never thought I would make it back from Iraq. Like Norwood Allman, my departure from a war zone was not well thought-out. I had little time to plan. But like him too, I was back in the U.S. I started to write this story, but since I no longer had the war as an excuse, the Illinois appellate court was not about to grant a continuance for anything less than an earthquake.

I stayed with a friend for the first few days and picked up the rest of the files. Beyond submitting the brief, I had no plan.

I wondered what had happened to my house on 46th Street. The house had been put up for sale, but as far as I knew it hadn't been sold. I drove to the neighborhood. The house was deserted. I went up to the front door—the plastic bag I had put over the light fixture to keep the rain off was still there. Surely a new buyer would have fixed the light—I had never been able to. I tried the key and it turned in the lock. Inside the power was on. There was an Internet connection. There was no hot water, but that could be fixed. One or two chairs were still in the front room. The futon was still there. It had either been too heavy to move or no one had wanted it. There was even a pillow. This was more than I had in Baghdad.

I started working on the brief. Three weeks later it was finished. I submitted it on time. Eighteen months later the appellate court upheld the sentence, but noted, at least, that my contribution at sentencing had reduced my client's sentence by twenty years. No greater reduction was warranted.

A few days after that I went to the Dade County courthouse to handle a hearing for a friend. The civil motion calendar is anything but thanks to attorneys who love to argue and judges who let them do so. The judges schedule dozens of matters for routine hearings at the same time. "Do we have a team yet?" is often heard in the halls, with the court clerks trying to round up attorneys who have more than one hearing scheduled for the same day at the same time. That way they can bill several clients for a single trip to the courthouse.

I reported in, waited for the other attorney to show up and then we both entered chambers. The other lawyer argued this point or that, and I sat impassively before telling the judge what my attorney-client's concerns were. The judge ruled. It was routine. Afterwards, the court reporter came up to me in the hall.

"Can I tell you something? You were so relaxed in there. I've never seen an attorney so relaxed."

I told her that I had just returned from Iraq. Compared to that, lawyers squabbling in Miami really was nothing. No one was shooting at you. What was called an emergency wasn't a real emergency. Compared to Iraq, there was nothing to really be worried about and my body language showed it.

A week later I was squatting in what had been my house wondering what to do next when the phone rang. It was an attorney in Toronto. "You don't know me," he said, "but I heard you used to practice in Saudi Arabia. We've just opened an office there. Would you like to go to Saudi Arabia?"

So now I come to the end of this Baghdad diary. I survived being in a war zone. I wasn't phased by it I thrived. It was a hardship but I enjoyed the thrill, the energy, the uncertainty. I enjoyed surviving, of waking up each morning and saying to myself, "I am alive."

Epilogue

THIS IS A TRUE STORY. Some names have been changed or withheld to protect the guilty or the innocent. Where appropriate, client names have been withheld in view of the attorney-client privilege.

As of the date of publication, MENA claims to have offices in Munich, Berlin, Baghdad, Cairo, Damascus, Dubai and Baghdad. There is no longer a separate office in what was the Green Zone.

Sabre Security is no longer in business in what was the Green Zone in Iraq. The Green Zone is no more.

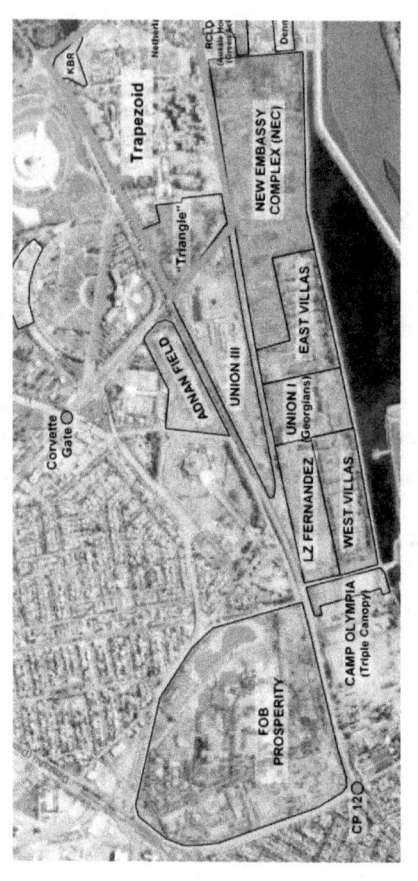

Green Zone map

This way to Baghdad

Personal Protective Equipment, or "PPE"

Please don't point your camera

Blast walls at night, Sabre compound, Interior

Sabre operations center

The office, early days

Sabre compound

The football field across the street from the Sabre compound

Bomb shelter on the football field

Sabre compound from across the street, showing blast walls and repurposed cargo containers

APPOINTMENT OF MILITARY POSTAL CLERK, UNIT MAIL CLERK OR MAIL ORDERLY (See Instructions on Reverse)	1. DATE EFFECTIVE	2. DATE REVOKED
	18 SEP	

3. NAME OF APPOINTEE (Last, First, Middle Initial)
OKANE MICHAEL

4. RANK OR GRADE	5. SSN	6. TITLE OF APPOINTEE
CIV	▇▇▇	UMC

7. ORGANIZATION/ACTIVITY	8. APO, MPO OR CONUS INSTALLATION
SABRE SECURITY	APO AE 09348

9. MAIL AUTHORIZED TO RECEIVE (Check and Initial)		10. THIS FORM MUST BE VALIDATED BY THE SERVING AGENCY'S GENERAL PURPOSE DATING STAMP PRIOR TO CLERK RECEIVING MAIL. IN THE CASE OF THE NAVY MOBILE UNITS, VALIDATION MAY BE BY IMPRESSION OF THE UNIT'S OFFICIAL SEAL
Personal (All) ☒ KK	Official (Except accountable) ☐	
Personal (Except accountable) ☐	Official Pouches Only ☐	
Official (All) ☒ KK		

SIGNATURE OF APPOINTING OFFICIAL	SIGNATURE OF APPOINTEE

DD Form 285, JUN 67

U.S. Navy postal clerk ID

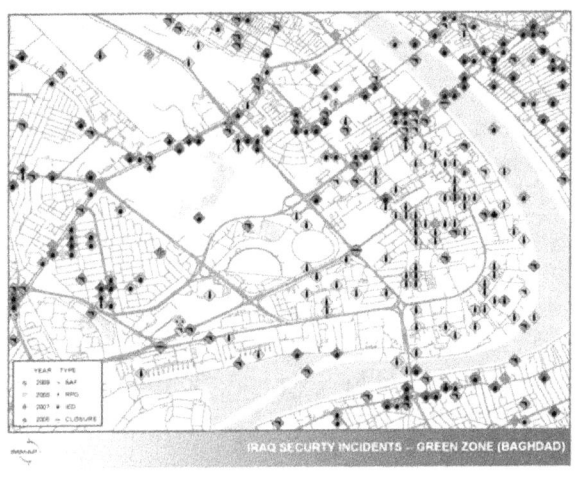

Security Incident Map

About the Author

MICHAEL O'KANE has practiced in Panama, Venezuela, Colombia, Saudi Arabia, Iraq, Bahrain and Bolivia. He has been involved in several high-profile matters such as *United States v. Noriega*, BCCI and the "British Bombers" case in Saudi Arabia. He is a former special legal advisor to the Kingdom of Saudi Arabia and in that capacity drafted a legal code for the Kingdom's Economic Cities project. His works include, *Doing Business in Saudi Arabia, Saudi Labor Law Outline, El pueblo and Miami Babilonia*. He has also translated José María Álvarez' *La esclava instruída* into English.

www.ingramcontent.com/pod-product-compliance
Lightning Source LLC
Chambersburg PA
CBHW050533300426
44113CB00012B/2073